Great Peasant Dishes of the World 🦢

Great
Peasant Dishes
of the World

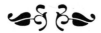

HOWARD HILLMAN

PROJECT COORDINATOR
Harriet Cohen

SPECIAL RESEARCH
Cherry Dumaual

HOUGHTON MIFFLIN COMPANY BOSTON
1983

Library of Congress Cataloging in Publication Data

Hillman, Howard.
    Great peasant dishes of the world.

    Includes index.
    1. Cookery, International. I. Title.
TX725.A1H5443 1983   641.59   82-15625
ISBN 0-395-32210-3

Printed in the United States of America

S 10 9 8 7 6 5 4 3 2 1

To the great peasant cooks of the world

Contents

Contents viii

Recipes by Categories

Country of Origin

AFGHANISTAN
Chae

ALGERIA
Harira

ARGENTINA
Empanadas

AUSTRIA
Speckknödel

BELGIUM
Carbonnade Flamande

BRAZIL
Vatapá

BULGARIA
Tarator

CHINA
Cha Chiang Mien
Hung Shao Chu Jou
Ching Yu

CUBA
Ropa Vieja

CZECHOSLOVAKIA
Houskové Knedlíky

DENMARK
Brunede Kartofler

ENGLAND
Blackberry Fool
Bubble and Squeak
Toad-in-the-Hole

EGYPT
Bamia

FINLAND
Karjalan Paisti

FRANCE
Cassoulet (Languedoc)
Choucroute Garnie (Alsace)
Côte de Porc Normande (Normandy)

PHILIPPINES
Adobo

POLAND
Pierogi

POLYNESIA
I'a Ota

PORTUGAL
Porco com Amêijoas

PUERTO RICO
Mofongo

REPUBLIC OF SOUTH AFRICA
Bobotie

RUMANIA
Mamaliga
Mititei

SCOTLAND
Scotch Broth

SENEGAL
Yassa

SOVIET UNION
Blini
Kissel

SPAIN
Arroz con Pollo
Bacalao a la Vizcaína
Sopa de Ajo

SRI LANKA
Malu Kiri

SWEDEN
Äppelkaka
Köttbullar

SWITZERLAND
Raclette

THAILAND
Tom Yam Kung

TURKEY
Yalanci Dolma

YUGOSLAVIA
Sarma

❧ Dishes for Entertaining

Bagna Cauda
Blackberry Fool
Blini
Bul-gogi
Couscous
Empanadas
Felafel
Houskové Knedlíky
Huachinango a la Veracruzano
Jollof Rice
Köttbullar
Mofongo
Mozzarella in Carrozza
Nasi Goreng
Osso Buco
Pierogi
Raclette
Tom Yam Kung

Tom Yam Kung
Vatapá

VEAL
Osso Buco

MIXED MEATS
Adobo (chicken and pork)
Cassoulet (pork and duck)
Jollof Rice (chicken and lamb)
Karjalan Paisti (beef, pork, and
   lamb)
Köttbullar (beef, veal, and pork)
Nasi Goreng (shrimp, pork, and
   chicken)
Porco com Amêijoas (pork and
   clams)

✌️§ Miscellaneous Categories

MEATLESS
Äppelkaka
Bamia
Blackberry Fool
Brunede Kartofler
Caponata
Chae
Ensalada de Aguacate y Tomate
Felafel
Gnocchi di Patate
Houskové Knedlíky
Huevos Rancheros
Kissel
Mamaliga
Mozzarella in Carrozza
Pesto
Raclette

Soda Bread
Somen
Sopa de Ajo
Tabbouleh
Tarator
Yalanci Dolma

HOT AND SPICY
Curried Kid
Ensalada de Aguacate y Tomate
Ground Nut Stew
Huevos Rancheros
Jollof Rice
Malu Kiri
Nasi Goreng
Papas con Salsa Queso
Roghan Josh
Tom Yam Kung
Vatapá
Yassa

**COOKING WITH ALCOHOLIC
BEVERAGES**
Arroz con Pollo
Bacalao a la Vizcaína
Carbonnade Flamande
Cassoulet
Choucroute Garnie
Cotriade
Côte de Porc Normande
Matelote à la Bourguignonne
Moules Marinière
Osso Buco
Porco com Amêijoas
Sauerbraten

FOR BARBECUES
Bul-gogi
Mititei

FOR BRUNCH
Blini
Caponata
Empanadas
Ensalada de Aguacate y Tomate
Fiskepudding
Hoppel Poppel
Huevos Rancheros
I'a Ota
Mamaliga
Mititei
Mozzarella in Carrozza
Oyako Donburi
Pierogi
Soda Bread
Somen
Toad-in-the-Hole

FOR GARLIC LOVERS
Adobo
Bagna Cauda
Bul-gogi
Mititei
Pesto
Sopa de Ajo
Tarator

FOR LATE-EVENING TREATS
Bagna Cauda
Raclette

FOR PICNICS
Äppelkaka
Caponata
Ensalada de Aguacate y Tomate
Pan Bagna
Rillettes

Soda Bread
Tabbouleh
Yalanci Dolma

FOR RICE LOVERS
Arroz con Pollo
Jollof Rice
Nasi Goreng
Oyako Donburi
Soupa Avgolemono
Yalanci Dolma

FOR USING LEFTOVER MEATS
Bubble and Squeak
Hoppel Poppel
Oyako Donburi

POPULAR WITH CHILDREN
Äppelkaka
Blackberry Fool
Brunede Kartofler
Bul-gogi
Cassoulet
Cha Chiang Mien
Empanadas
Erwtensoep
Felafel
Fiskepudding
Hoppel Poppel
Houskové Knedlíky
Kissel
Köttbullar
Mozzarella in Carrozza
Pan Bagna
Pierogi
Raclette
Toad-in-the-Hole

**RELATIVELY SIMPLE TO
PREPARE**
Bagna Cauda
Blackberry Fool
Brunede Kartofler
Bul-gogi
Caponata
Chae
Ching Yu
Côte de Porc Normande
Ensalada de Aguacate y Tomate
Erwtensoep
Hoppel Poppel
I'a Ota
Kissel

Malu Kiri
Mamaliga
Mozzarella in Carrozza
Oyako Donburi
Papas con Salsa Queso
Raclette
Soda Bread
Somen
Sopa de Ajo
Soupa Avgolemono
Tabbouleh
Toad-in-the-Hole
Tom Yam Kung
Yassa

Introduction

❧ Peasant dishes are delicious. That's why I want to share with you some of my favorite recipes, ones I learned from peasant cooks during my various gastronomic journeys around the world. Each of these recipes is, of course, authentic and kitchen-tested.

What is a peasant? In the context of this book, a peasant is a small-scale farmer, rancher, herder, hunter, or fisherman. Unlike the city dweller, the peasant is close to his food source.

By no means is a peasant necessarily impoverished. As with the members of the urban working class, some peasants are nearly destitute but others have sufficient resources to prepare interesting and high-quality dishes. My book concentrates on the best of peasant cookery.

Anthropologists tell us that the peasant class came into being some ten thousand years ago, with the birth of agriculture. The first peasants were, in the words of Daniel Webster, "the founders of civilization."

Until fairly recently, practically everyone was a peasant. Though a small, steady stream of peasants was migrating to the towns, the big exodus didn't begin until the dawn of the Industrial Revolution in the eighteenth century. Farmers, forsaking the soil, flocked to urban centers to search for jobs in factories. Nevertheless, peasants still account for most of the world's population.

You probably have more peasant ancestors who've lived since the time when Columbus discovered America than you might imagine. Because there have been roughly twenty-five generations of your forebears since 1492, you have — mathematically — thirty-three million direct ancestors (parents, grandparents, great-grandparents, and so on) who have walked on the earth during the past five hundred years. Unless your blood is as pure blue and aristocratic as that of Prince Charles, millions of your progenitors were peasants.

All the classical cuisines of the world — including those of France, Italy, and China — have their roots in peasant dishes. The same is true for most of the bourgeois, or urban middle-class, dishes.

A few dishes that traveled to the city have crossed international boundaries, as is the case with stuffed vine leaves. Though the Turkish version, *yalanci dolma,* is the original, you can't blame the Greeks for thinking that stuffed vine leaves are their creation. When one's grandmother's grandmother made them, how could anyone think otherwise?

Some ingredients, such as carrots, are becoming global staples. Where the French have been, I've seen thyme in the native marketplaces. The onion family, of course, has always been a universal flavoring agent.

Because dishes do cross borders, it is difficult and sometimes impossible to determine with any degree of certainty the true homeland of some peasant creations. Scant evidence exists because ethnic groups migrate and frontiers change. Just as important, written records are rare on this subject. Peasant cooks seldom, if ever, jotted down recipes, and the ancient scribes in the city almost never chronicled for posterity the dishes that peasants ate.

In my experience, peasants possess a greater sense of sharing than city dwellers. Generally, peasants offer their hospitality more quickly and graciously. Personal and group integrity also tends to be stronger among the peasantry. As Cato the Elder observed in 200 B.C., "Farmers are, of all men, the least given to vice." This value is ingrained in the peasants' way of life, because there are fewer people for them to depend on in times of adversity. Firm and lasting bonds must be made with neighbors.

Religion — and folk tradition in general — is more closely tied to the eating ritual. It is not uncommon, for example, for the women in a peasant household to spend several days before a holiday preparing the dishes of their ancestors.

Peasants unconsciously use their culinary traditions to identify themselves with their peer group — and to exclude outsiders from membership in their group. Their unique cuisine gives them psychological reassurance that they are a special people. Thus peasants are less likely to try a new food. In fact, in recent times, thousands of peasants in Asia and Africa starved because they refused to eat the unfamiliar ingredients imported by relief agencies.

When it comes to familiar foods, peasants are more economy-minded than their city brethren. A country cook in China will, as the saying goes, use everything but the squeal of a pig.

Peasants are more self-sufficient — the more isolated their homestead, the more this seems to be true. I've noticed that peasants tend to view the land not so much as a means of generating income, but as an intrinsic aspect of life itself. Not only do peasants develop a deep emotional attachment to the soil that furnishes their livelihood, they also focus most of their thoughts and hopes on that small piece of real estate.

Labor is divided on the basis of age and sex, and children start pulling their own weight at an early age. The five-year-old peasant son is more apt to be working in the fields than playing in the back yard. The daughter starts learning her mother's unwritten recipes as soon as she is old enough to hold on to the proverbial apron strings. Culinary tradition is thus passed down from generation to generation.

My book will help you learn part of this culinary tradition because each recipe accurately captures the dish as I've learned to cook it in peasant homes. Unlike many of the ethnic cookbooks written by armchair gourmets, my volume is based on firsthand experiences.

In only a few instances have I been forced to alter a traditional peasant recipe in order to adapt it to the American kitchen — and even then, it was changed to such a minor extent that the authenticity of the dish was not violated.

I automatically excluded some of my favorite dishes from this book whenever a certain ingredient, essential to the character of the preparation, was not available in stateside ethnic stores or through reliable mail-order sources. For example, I have the recipe for a savory Nepalese stew. Unfortunately, it requires yak butter, a fat that is probably available in this country only through your local zoo keeper.

Other dishes were omitted because the cooking technique cannot be adequately described in words. Many arts, such as the making of strudel dough, are best learned in the presence of a teacher, be she your grandmother or a cooking-school instructor.

I have steered clear of American peasant recipes (the one exception being *mofongo,* from Puerto Rico). That subject demands a different editorial approach as well as an entire book of its own (I will be writing that volume in the future). If I had randomly selected a few of the many regional American recipes, I would have been besieged by outraged readers complaining, "Why didn't you include a recipe from my particular area?" Regrettably, there's only so much space in one book, so I restricted myself to peasant recipes from foreign lands. That's a tall order as it is.

I've limited the number of recipes so that I could concentrate on quality rather than quantity (more than a few cookbooks take the opposite approach, presenting five hundred mediocre recipes instead of a few good ones). Even though the number of recipes in this book is relatively small, there are enough to keep you happily cooking for a year and a half if you try one new recipe a week. The recipes range from the simple (*bagna cauda,* for instance) to the complex (*cassoulet,* for example). Whatever their degree of difficulty, these peasant dishes share a common characteristic: They're tasty and worth the effort.

I've given detailed instructions because it takes far less time to read an explicit recipe than it does to cook a doomed dish. (As one who has taught cooking classes, I know all too well how the omission of a guideline can sometimes stymie the efforts of even good cooks.) My other goal in providing in-depth recipes is to share with you various tips. Consider this book a cooking lesson.

Some of the recipes call for many ingredients. Since most of them can be measured and combined ahead of time, the recipes are not as complicated as they might seem at first glance.

You will probably notice that many soups, stews, and casseroles are included, which is as it should be. Peasants cook such dishes very often. Some of the preparations require cooking the slow, old-fashioned way: They sit for hours on the stove or in the oven. You need not worry about spending hours in the kitchen, though, for pot tending is at a minimum.

This book contains a limited number of desserts because that course is not common in most peasant homes.

Four of the recipes in this book — *csirke paprikás* (chicken paprika), *sauerbraten,* Scotch broth, and soda bread — can be found in almost any general cookbook. I included them because many of the available recipes for these specialties do not produce the satisfactory results that these dishes deserve. Prove it to yourself. Try, for example, the peasant recipe for *csirke paprikás* and compare the results with the other chicken paprikas that you've eaten. I think you will be pleasantly surprised.

Though my recipes are authentic, there are other equally authentic but different versions — as many as there are cooks. I've often sampled a rendition of a specific ethnic specialty in one hut, only to find a markedly different concoction in the dwelling next door. Peasant cooks, by and large, enjoy making a popular dish their own by giving it a unique twist. Only a purist far removed from the farm would insist on a rigid formula. Besides, cooking a recipe the same way twice is not being creative.

There is nothing wrong and much good to say about customizing an authentic peasant recipe to suit your palate and whim. However, should your variations alter the spirit of the dish, then please — for the sake of gastronomy — rename the creation. A cook dilutes the meaning of a name when, for example, he or she marinates beef for only twenty-four hours, yet insists on calling the preparation *sauerbraten.* Such a short marinating period does not impart the desired sour (*sauer*) flavor to the meat. Nor does it sufficiently break down the connective tissue to make the cut of beef as tender as it should be.

To encourage you to try different ways of cooking the recipes in this book the second time you try them, I have included within each recipe a section called Variations on a Theme.

Be creative, but remember that you will sacrifice quality if you don't adhere to certain basic cooking principles. For instance: You shouldn't rush the cooking process — if a recipe calls for simmering as opposed to boiling, or for cooking the food over low heat or in a 300° F oven, do it. If you have doubts about the precision of your oven temperature dial (most are shamefully inaccurate), buy a good oven thermometer. Be sure your kitchen timer is accurate, too. Always read a recipe thoroughly and with understanding before you plow into it. If a recipe or technique is new to you, allot more time than you think you might need.

Buy and use top-quality ingredients — and, when applicable, the freshest ones. If you cook with meat or seafood that has been frozen, you will suffer the consequence: Your ingredient will lose much of its desirable flavor and texture. Never use those abominable-tasting "convenience" foods such as garlic powder and bottled lemon juice (the very thought of them makes me cringe). Cooks who live in large cities should be able to buy all of the ingredients called for in the recipes of this book. Some readers will not be as fortunate. For those recipes with ingredients that might be hard to find locally, I present a mail-order section.

Nearly 20 percent of the dishes in this book are hot and spicy because many peasant cuisines use chili in abundance. The more you eat chilies over a period of time, the more you develop an immunity to their fiery wallop (I discuss that subject more fully in my book *Kitchen Science*). If you don't eat chilies often, cut down the quantity called for in the recipe (but not to the point where the dish loses its intended character). If you've already built up a solid immunity to chili, then perhaps you'll want to increase the quantity called for in the recipe — but remember to take into account the immunities of the other people who will be dining at your table. Also be aware that the hotness of chili varies by species, region, and season.

I highly recommend that you search out peasant dishes on your next trip abroad. It's an excellent way to meet people who live in the countryside. Expressing a genuine interest in someone's food is one of the quickest ways to win a heart. Take Spain, for instance. If you go to the hinterland and tell the typical peasant that you enjoy reading the works of the Spanish author Juan Valera, you won't arouse his interest. If, on the other hand, you tell him that you enjoy one of the peasant dishes of his region, his eyes will gleam.

There are several ways to meet peasant cooks. One of my methods is to ask a friend or acquaintance who lives in the country I am visiting to arrange a trip to the home of a skilled peasant cook (not all peasants are good cooks, mind you).

Another approach is to ask the country's consulate or tourist agency in the United States to arrange the get-together before you leave home. Be on guard when using this method, however, because most governmental bodies — if they decide to help you at all — will often set you up with a member of the upper class who seldom cooks (she employs a servant cook). Usually, this type of person pretends to others (and sometimes to herself) that she knows more about the local peasant dishes than she actually does. Should this woman be an accomplished cook, she will probably show you how to make the dish with a cosmopolitan accent, convinced that you wouldn't like the authentic native version.

The governmental arm may also try to give you the name of a restaurant that serves some peasant dishes. Your chance of learning how to cook a peasant dish authentically in one of these establishments is remote. Anyone who has worked in a restaurant, as I have, knows that the establishment — if it is to pay its rent — usually cannot afford to take the time-consuming traditional steps that spell the difference between a merely acceptable peasant dish and a superb one.

I find that one of the best ways to meet a peasant cook is to hop in a car, drive through the dirt roads of the countryside, make inquiries, and leave fate to serendipity. It works — most of the time, at least. If I can't rent, borrow, or steal a car, I try to find a local cab driver who is related to a great peasant cook. I then do my best to negotiate a fair rate for him to drive me to his relative's home. The trip turns out to be a one-day paid vacation for the driver to visit his relatives in the country and a splendid opportunity for me to learn more about peasant cooking.

What about the language barrier? Naturally, it would be nice to know how to speak the local tongue in each region of the world, but since there are five thousand ethnic groups with populations of at least one million that have their own dialects, there is no way for anyone to master all of them. Although I speak English (the best all-around language for international travel) and "survival" French, German, and Spanish, I'm still literally at a loss for words in many parts of the world. Even if I mastered Mandarin, I still would not be able to converse with the majority of the people in China — they speak different dialects. Therefore, it's essential to develop back-up methods to help overcome the Tower of Babel predicament.

Obviously, the best solution — short of learning the dialect — is to bring along someone who can translate for you. If that is not possible, tote along a good dictionary and phrase book, complete with a pronunciation guide. Also carry with you various letters of introduction that explain — in the local dialect — your goals and motives. It's always easier to cajole someone into writing these messages for you if you supply the pen and paper.

You'll also have to rely on body language, the means of communication that has been used since the days of Herodotus, Marco Polo, and other early explorers. The more you travel to exotic lands, the more adept you become at this nonverbal skill. I'm always amazed at how much a seasoned traveler can say with simple gestures and heartfelt smiles.

When you find a recipe for a great peasant dish, don't forget to send me a copy. I would love to try it.

Howard Hillman

Appetizers

᷒ Bagna Cauda   *Serves 4 to 8*
(BAHN-yah COW-dah)

I had the good fortune of being in the right place at the right time during the fall grape harvest in the Piedmont region of northern Italy. As I was observing the workers gathering the grapes in a photogenic vineyard, the owner drove up the dusty dirt road. He stepped out of his truck, clutching a surprise: an earthenware crock half-filled with a hot olive-oil-and-butter sauce, accented with anchovies and garlic. He also brought half a dozen liter bottles of hearty red wine and two wicker baskets — one overflowing with bread sticks and the other with fresh, raw vegetables, including scallions and cardoon stalks. All was neatly placed on a grassy patch under a venerable oak tree.

The workers quickly assembled themselves around the fare, leaving a sitting space for me. Without hesitation I accepted their implicit offer.

Bagna cauda (literally, "hot sauce") is finger food. Following the lead of my new-found friends, I selected a vegetable, dipped it in the hot sauce, and savored the morsel. After quaffing some of the wine, I dipped into the sauce my next food choice, a crusty bread stick for which Piedmontese bakers are famous. With a little practice, I was able to transfer each piece of food to my mouth without allowing a single drop of the clinging sauce to fall in my lap.

Some Piedmontese, like my host in the vineyard, serve *bagna cauda* as a meal in itself. Other local citizens offer it to their guests as an appetizer or late-evening snack.

Vegetables (see below)	2 tablespoons finely minced
Bread sticks	garlic
¾ cup olive oil	3 tablespoons chopped
4 tablespoons unsalted butter	anchovies

Steps

1. Prepare the vegetables and arrange them attractively on a platter (preferably earthenware). Place the bread sticks upright in a straight-sided earthenware container. Bring the two dishes to the table.
2. Add the oil, butter, garlic, and anchovies to a shallow 1- to 1½-quart flame-proof pot. Heat the mixture to 200° F and maintain that temperature for 10 minutes.
3. Bring the pot to the table and place it over a warming unit (such as a candle warmer, Sterno or spirit lamp, or electric hot plate). Enjoy, as described in the introduction to this recipe.

Vegetable Choices

Serve a color-contrasting medley of some of these or other suitable vegetables:

Artichoke hearts and leaves (cooked)	Cucumber strips
	Endive leaves
Arugula leaves	Fennel stalks
Asparagus (parboiled)	Jerusalem artichokes
Broccoli florets	Mushrooms
Cabbage leaves	Parsnips
Cardoon stalks	Radishes
Carrot sticks	Scallions
Cauliflower florets	Spinach leaves
Celery stalks	Sweet pepper rings or strips
Cherry tomatoes	

If you're splurging, consider using white truffles.

Additional Keys to Success

It is unnecessary to crisp the vegetables in ice water in the refrigerator if your vegetables are fresh to begin with, which they should be. ¶ Be selective. It is better to have only two or three very fresh vegetables than it is to have an array of tired ones. ¶ The pot for cooking and serving the sauce should be sufficiently attractive to bring to the table. Ideal would be an earthenware chafing dish (such as a small fondue pot). ¶ The oil must not get too hot. Otherwise, it might burn the garlic and butter or, worse, the diners' lips and mouth lining.

Don't use the simmer criterion to determine 200° F, because you are dealing with a fat rather than a water medium. Your best bet is to use a suitable thermometer.

Serving Suggestions and Affinities

Bagna cauda is best during the nonsummer months. ¶ Open a hearty and heady red wine, such as Barbera, from the Piedmont region. ¶ Follow your casual *bagna cauda* feast with oranges or another acidic fruit.

Variation on a Theme

Add heavy cream in step 2, but keep the temperature below 170° F and stir frequently to prevent the cream from curdling.

⊸§ Blini   *Serves 4 to 8*
(BLEE-neh)

Before the 1917 Russian Revolution, the Orthodox Church greatly influenced the eating customs of the peasantry, particularly during the forty days of Lent. The devoted would, in effect, become vegetarians because their religion demanded complete abstinence from meat, fish, eggs, and dairy products, including butter.

With a restricted diet to look forward to, it was understandable that the Russians would want to go on an eating binge before the forty-day ban took effect. They did. The peasants celebrated a week-long carnival called Maslenista — literally, "butter festival." Merry-making was rampant, but the focus was on the *blin* (or, in the plural, *blini*). This yeast-raised pancake was fried in devilish quantities of butter and then "sinfully" spread with even more butter. Next came a topping, or two or three, on each *blin* — perhaps smoked salmon or any of the other items I list in the Serving Suggestions and Affinities section of the recipe.

Only a very small percentage of Russians still follows the faith. The nonbelievers, however, still carry on with delight the annual pre-Lenten tradition of Maslenista. I've met many a Russian who eats a dozen well-garnished *blini* in one sitting while periodically tossing down the hatch, in a single gulp, a shot of icy vodka. I suspect this gastronomic orgy of the Russians will last for at least another thousand years.

1⅔ cups whole milk	⅓ cup lukewarm water
3 large eggs	1 cup buckwheat flour
4 tablespoons unsalted butter	1 cup white flour
1 package active dry yeast	½ teaspoon salt (or to taste)
1 tablespoon sugar	

Steps

1. Bring the milk and eggs to room temperature. Melt the butter with very low heat (as over the pilot-light area of your range).
2. Dissolve the yeast and sugar in the water. Let the mixture rest for 5 to 8 minutes.
3. Separate the eggs.
4. Blend the two flours and the salt in a bowl. Form the mixture into a mound and shape a well in its center.
5. Place in the well the yeast mixture, the milk, the egg yolks, and 3 tablespoons of the melted (but not hot) butter. Blend the ingredients with a wooden spoon. Use a circular motion, starting slowly at first, then gradually increasing your speed.
6. Cover the bowl with a kitchen towel and let the batter stand in a warm (about 85° F), draft-free spot for approximately 40 to 60 minutes, or until the batter doubles in volume.
7. Preheat the oven to 200° F.
8. Whip the egg whites to the stiff-peak stage. Gently fold the foam into the batter. Cover the batter and return it to its resting spot for another 20 to 30 minutes.
9. Heat a griddle, or one or more thick-bottomed skillets. When it is hot, lightly brush the surface with the remaining melted butter.
10. Ladle onto the griddle 3 tablespoons of the batter for each *blin*, allowing at least 1 inch of space between each one. When the top of each *blin* is amply covered with small bubbles, turn it and cook for approximately 2 more minutes.
11. Stack the cooked *blini* on a warm platter. Cover them with a kitchen towel and keep them warm in the oven until you have prepared a sufficient quantity of *blini* for the first helping. (Keep the remaining batter covered until you are ready to cook the next round.) Remove the *blini* from the oven and serve promptly.

Additional Keys to Success

Lukewarm is 110° to 115° F. If the water is too cold, the yeast won't multiply. If the water is too hot, the yeast will die. ¶ Your yeast is dead or debilitated if the mixture in step 2 doesn't become bubbly after the 5- to 8-minute period. ¶ The sugar is necessary because it serves as nourishment for the yeast in step 2. It also caramelizes during the cooking step and thereby gives the surface of each *blin* a desirable rich, brown hue. ¶ If you use refrigerator-cold milk and eggs, the rising process will be retarded. ¶ The temperature inside a gas oven that is heated only by its pilot light is usually about 85° F. If you must let the batter rise at room temperature (68° to 72° F), then allow an additional 20 to 30 minutes in step 6 for the batter to double in volume. Also allow an additional 10 to 15 minutes in step 8. ¶ Egg whites whip better if they are at room temperature. ¶ To test the griddle for proper hotness, dribble a few small drops of water on top of it. When the droplets begin to "dance" on the griddle, it will be sufficiently hot in a couple of minutes. *Blini* should be about 3½ to 4 inches in diameter; whatever size you choose, they should be uniform. ¶ As with all pancakes, the first set of *blini* to come off the griddle will likely be inferior. Be prepared to toss that lot to your pet. ¶ The *blini* will become unnecessarily dry if they are kept in the oven for more than 10 minutes.

Serving Suggestions and Affinities

Blini are not meant to be eaten alone. By far the most popular toppings are butter and, especially, sour cream. Many Russians first brush the *blin* with melted butter, then spoon on a portion of caviar, salmon roe, smoked fish, salted herring, or pickled vegetables, then crown their creation with a small dollop of sour cream. Sometimes the buttered *blini* are smeared with a sweet — a jam, jelly, or preserve. ¶ Vodka, neat and ice cold, is the traditional beverage accompaniment. Brut champagne is another good choice because it, like the vodka, helps cut through the butter, sour cream, and other fatty toppings.

Variations on a Theme

Use a higher or lower ratio of buckwheat to white flour to suit your taste. However, if you reduce the buckwheat proportion too much,

you won't have peasant-style *blini.* ¶ Some recipes call for several
risings of the batter.

Mail-Order Sources

Buckwheat flour is available through the mail from H. Roth & Son,
1577 First Avenue, New York, New York 10028 (212-734-1110). Caviar is available from Caviarteria, 29 East 60th Street, New York, New
York 10022 (212-759-7410; outside New York State use the toll-free
number, 800-221-1020).

⁓§ Caponata   *Serves 4 to 6*
(kah-poh-NAH-tah)

Sicily is a raw land of sweeping beauty, from the snowy slopes of
Mount Etna to the sun-drenched Mediterranean coast ringing the
island. Even on my first day in Sicily I sensed a mystical electricity
in the air, one that seems to charge the inhabitants with a lust for
life and food.

If one local dish reflects this feeling, it would have to be *caponata.*
I learned my favorite recipe for it from a grandmother who was born
and reared in a village twenty miles beyond the city limits of Palermo.
In front of me in her orderly kitchen she pulled from her market
basket some yellow onions, with their green stalks attached, eggplants
no longer than my index finger, and ripe tomatoes kissed by the
fierce Sicilian sun. Hidden in the recesses of her cupboard were the
other ingredients needed for her special *caponata.* The pine nuts were
crisp; her olive oil was redolent of the countryside.

After watching her prepare the *caponata,* I asked the woman for
a sample. To my surprise, she wouldn't let me taste even the smallest
morsel. "It won't be at its best till this evening," she explained. "Come
back then." I did, with no regrets. By nightfall the individual flavors
of the various ingredients had commingled into a unified aria of sheer
gustatory bliss.

You will no doubt notice a similarity between the *caponata* of
Sicily and the *ratatouille* of Provence. Both dishes are made with
eggplants, tomatoes, olive oil, and a melody of flavoring agents. My
taste buds admire both dishes, but I believe that the Sicilian one
has a flavor more evocative of the peasant kitchen.

1 pound baby eggplants
⅓ cup olive oil
½ cup sliced yellow onions
½ teaspoon minced garlic
⅓ cup diced inner celery stalks
1 cup peeled and quartered
  Italian plum tomatoes
2 tablespoons drained whole
  capers

2 tablespoons chopped fresh
  parsley
¼ teaspoon salt (or to taste)
⅛ teaspoon freshly ground black
  pepper
¼ teaspoon red pepper flakes
3 tablespoons white vinegar
2 teaspoons sugar
2 tablespoons pine nuts

Steps

1. Stem the eggplants. Quarter them lengthwise and then cut the pieces into ¾-inch chunks.
2. Heat the olive oil in a large, heavy-bottomed sauté pan over low to moderate heat.
3. Cook the eggplant chunks in a single loose layer for 5 minutes, stirring frequently. (If you don't have a large sauté pan, cook the eggplant in batches.)
4. Transfer the eggplant with a slotted spoon to a warm bowl.
5. Adjust the heat to low and sauté the onions for 1 minute, stirring frequently. Add the garlic and sauté for 1 minute, stirring frequently. Add the celery and sauté for 1 minute, stirring frequently.
6. Return the eggplant to the pan. Stir in the tomatoes, capers, parsley, salt, pepper, red pepper flakes, vinegar, and sugar. Bring the preparation to a simmer. Cover and gently simmer the mixture for 10 minutes, stirring occasionally.
7. Stir in the pine nuts. Turn off the heat and let the *caponata* partially cool. Transfer it to a bowl. Cover and refrigerate it for at least half a day. Remove it from the refrigerator 1 hour before serving.

Additional Keys to Success

To make a worthy *caponata,* you need baby eggplants, the kind that are less than 5 inches long. ❡ It is not necessary to soak baby eggplants in salted water. (As for the larger eggplants customarily sold in supermarkets, not even the soaking process will expunge their pronounced bitterness.) ❡ After washing the eggplants, be sure to pat them dry. Otherwise, the clinging water will splatter in the hot oil. ❡ If fresh, vine-ripened Italian plum tomatoes are unavailable, substitute a good brand of canned imported Italian tomatoes. Discard the water from the can. ¶ The skins of the fresh tomatoes will easily peel off if you first parboil the tomatoes for 30 to 60 seconds (depending on their variety) and then quickly submerge them in cold tap water. ¶ Good brands of olive oil, vinegar, and capers are essential to the success of this dish. ¶ During step 6, do not overcook or too forcefully stir the mixture. Otherwise, your *caponata* will become a purée because the eggplant chunks will overly soften and the tomato quarters will totally disintegrate.

Serving Suggestions and Affinities

Serve individual portions in ramekins or on lettuce leaves. ¶ *Caponata* may be featured as an appetizer, part of an antipasto, a vegetable side dish or salad (but never as the main entrée, since it is incredibly rich), or as a topping for slices of crusty bread. ¶ *Caponata* is particularly delightful on a hot summer day. ¶ For a change of pace, serve *caponata* hot on a cool evening.

Variations on a Theme

Experiment with additions such an anchovies, black or green olives, and Italian green peppers.

Leftovers

Because of its relatively high acid content, leftover *caponata* will keep for at least a week if covered and refrigerated.

Mail-Order Source

Pine nuts are available through the mail from Karnig Tashjian, 380 Third Avenue, New York, New York 10016 (212-683-8458).

◄§ Empanadas   *Serves 4*
(em-pah-NAH-thahs)

Empanadas are small baked turnovers typically filled with seasoned ground or chopped meat. They are popular throughout the Argentine pampas from the southern Atlantic coast to the foothills of the Andes. This specialty has also become a staple in several other South American countries.

Farmers and ranchers on the pampas relish *empanadas* as much for their convenience as for their savoriness. They can be toted to work in the fields and grazing lands, and eaten out of hand as a snack or midday meal.

One of the many Argentineans I saw devouring *empanadas* on the job was a gaucho, the local equivalent of an American cowboy and, like his counterpart, a vanishing breed. His outfit was most traditional, from his dark felt hat to his high-heeled boots. His baggy white trousers were secured by a wide leather belt and he wore a scarf around his neck and a wool poncho over his shoulders. Hanging from his saddle was a bola, a weapon consisting of two heavy balls tied to opposite ends of a long thong and used to entangle the legs of cattle.

This handsome gaucho was munching on an *empanada* while waving the herd through a gate with his free hand. He seemed to be enjoying the *empanada* so much that I asked the ranch cook for a sample. Two bites later I was asking, if not begging, him for this recipe.

¼ pound unsalted butter
2 cups all-purpose flour
1 teaspoon baking powder
½ teaspoon salt (or to taste)
2 yolks of large eggs
¼ cup chilled water
1 tablespoon vegetable oil
½ pound ground lean beef

½ cup chopped white onions
2 tablespoons seedless raisins
2 tablespoons chopped black or
  green olives
½ teaspoon ground red pepper
  (cayenne)
½ teaspoon oregano
½ teaspoon salt

Steps

1. Cut the butter into ¼-inch cubes.
2. Place the flour, baking powder, salt, and butter in a mixing bowl. Combine the ingredients with a pastry cutter (or with the steel blade in a food processor).
3. Beat the egg yolks. Mix half of them into the flour mixture. Reserve the remainder for step 12.
4. Incorporate the water slowly into the flour mixture until the dough becomes a cohesive and semifirm mass.

5. Shape the dough into two balls. Wrap them in plastic wrap and refrigerate them for 15 minutes.

6. Preheat the oven to 375° F.

7. Heat the oil in a large sauté pan or skillet over moderate heat. Sauté the meat for 3 minutes, stirring frequently. Transfer the meat with a slotted spoon to a warm bowl.

8. Add the onions to the pan and sauté them over low to moderate heat for 3 minutes, stirring frequently. (Add 1 or 2 extra teaspoons of oil if necessary.)

9. Return the meat to the pan and add the remaining ingredients. Cook the mixture for 1 minute, stirring constantly. Reserve it for step 11.

10. Roll each ball of dough on a lightly floured board into a ⅛-inch-thick sheet. Using a cookie cutter with a 4- to 5-inch diameter, cut out rounds. Collect the scraps and repeat step 10 until the dough is used up.

11. Place 1 tablespoon of the meat mixture in the center of each dough round. Lightly moisten the exposed dough with cold tap water. Fold each round in half, creating a half-moon shape. Crimp the two edges of the dough together so that the stuffing cannot ooze out during the baking step.

12. Brush the tops of the uncooked *empanadas* with the remaining egg yolk.

13. Place the uncooked *empanadas* on an ungreased baking sheet. Bake them in the middle of the oven until the tops become light golden brown (roughly 20 minutes). Serve the *empanadas* fresh from the oven.

Additional Keys to Success

Do not mix the ingredients in step 2 into a smooth mass. Stop your task as soon as the flour-coated butter particles are slightly smaller than ⅛ inch thick. ¶ If your flour is particularly dry, you might have to add a little more chilled water than called for in the recipe. ¶ Do not omit the raisins from the recipe; they are needed to absorb excess liquid from the stuffing during the baking step. ¶ If you do not have a 4- or 5-inch cookie cutter, use the rim of a suitably sized glass or empty can. ¶ In step 11, you can crimp the dough with either your fingers (for a wavy pattern) or the tines of a fork.

Serving Suggestions and Affinities

Empanadas can be presented as appetizers for a dinner or as the star item for a light lunch or snack. ¶ *Empanadas* are perfect for picnics. ¶ Serve a young, robust dry wine or chilled beer.

Variations on a Theme

Use lard rather than butter. ¶ Prepare chicken, shrimp, cheese, or vegetable *empanadas.* ¶ Experiment with additions such as diced sweet peppers, crumbled hard-cooked eggs, minced garlic, or herbs of your choice. ¶ Make smaller *empanadas* and call them *empanaditas.* ¶ For a browner crust, add a little sugar in step 2. ¶ Deep-fry your *empanadas.* ¶ Top your *empanadas* with tomato (or other) sauce.

✌ Felafel   *Serves 6 to 8*
(feh-LAH-fehl)

Felafel are deep-fried balls of ground chickpeas blended with a little bulgur wheat. "Kosher pork balls" is how one Israeli humorously described this meatless treat to me. When they come out of the hot oil, crisp and brown, *felafel* can be eaten as hors d'oeuvres, or popped into halved pita bread along with some salad and a fiery sauce.

Felafel is not unique to Israel. I've sampled this food throughout most of the Middle East, and I suspect its peasant origins go far back in time. Neither is *felafel* strictly rural fare — it has become a popular snack sold by street vendors in all of Israel's largest cities.

I found my favorite recipe for *felafel* in a small kibbutz near the Sea of Galilee. As with other kibbutzim, life on this self-sufficient farm was communal. The members jointly owned the property and shared the fruits of their labor. They even ate most of their meals together in a large, spic-and-span dining room staffed by their fellow kibbutzniks.

"Pity the kibbutz chef who can't make a good *felafel,*" explained one of the cooks in the kitchen, sporting a twinkle in her eye. "If we can't make our friends a decent *felafel,* out we go to hoeing weeds and digging ditches."

½ pound dried chickpeas

¼ cup bulgur (cracked wheat)

⅓ cup unseasoned bread crumbs

¼ cup sliced scallions

1 teaspoon minced garlic

1 teaspoon ground cumin

1 tablespoon fresh lemon juice

2 teaspoons crushed dried mint

½ teaspoon ground red pepper (cayenne)

½ teaspoon salt (or to taste)

2 yolks of large eggs

Vegetable oil for deep-frying

Steps

1. Soak the chickpeas overnight in four times their volume of cold tap water in a noncorrosible bowl. Change the water at least once.
2. Drain the chickpeas and put them in a large pot; add enough cold tap water to cover them by 1 inch. Bring the liquid to a simmer and cook for 1 hour.
3. Soak the bulgur for 10 minutes in ⅓ cup of cold tap water; drain thoroughly.
4. Drain the chickpeas thoroughly.
5. Purée the chickpeas, bulgur, and the remaining ingredients (except the vegetable oil) in a food processor, using the steel blade, or in an electric blender. If you need to purée the mixture in two or more batches, use proportionate amounts of ingredients.
6. Form the paste into compact 1-inch balls, using moistened hands. Place them on a plate in one layer, being careful to space the balls so they are not touching. Set aside at room temperature for 1 hour.
7. Preheat to 370° F vegetable oil several inches deep in a deep-fryer or another wide pan.
8. In batches, deep-fry the balls in the hot oil for about 3 minutes, or until golden brown.
9. With a slotted spoon, transfer the cooked *felafel* to paper towels. Pat the *felafel* dry. Serve them hot.

Additional Keys to Success

Substitute canned chickpeas for the more flavorful dried variety only if necessary. ¶ Do not soak the bulgur for longer than 10 minutes or in more than ⅓ cup of water. This grain must still have some water-absorption capacity when you blend it with the other ingredients. ¶ If bulgur is unavailable, use an extra ¼ cup of bread crumbs or 2 tablespoons of flour. ¶ If possible, prepare the bread crumbs from slightly stale pita bread. ¶ Don't guess the oil's temperature — use a deep-frying thermometer. If the temperature is much more than 370° F, the exterior of the *felafel* will burn before the core has been properly heated. If the temperature is much below 370° F, the *felafel* paste will absorb a lot of oil and therefore become greasy. ¶ Since the *felafel* balls are delicately bound together, it is highly advisable to cook them in a deep-frying wire basket. ¶ Do not crowd the pan in step 8. Adding too many *felafel* at a time will drastically reduce the temperature of the cooking oil and cause the *felafel* to become greasy.

Serving Suggestions and Affinities

Offer your guests *felafel* as hors d'oeuvres. ¶ Arrange the *felafel* in a single layer on a warm plate and skewer them with toothpicks. Alternatively, mound the *felafel* in a warm bowl and serve the toothpicks on the side. ¶ Prepare a dipping sauce for the *felafel*. Possibilities include sauces with a yogurt, tomato, or tahini (sesame paste) base.

Variations on a Theme

For lighter-textured *felafel*, use ¼ to ½ teaspoon baking powder. ¶ Chickpeas by themselves are relatively bland and therefore need seasoning. This characteristic gives you the opportunity to experiment by using herbs and spices of your choice. ¶ Make *felafel* the old-fashioned way: with a mortar and pestle. ¶ Shape the *felafel* paste into rolls or disks. ¶ Stuff one or more *felafel* into pita bread and finish filling the cavity with salad greens coated with tahini, or use diced fresh vegetables such as cucumbers and tomatoes.

Mail-Order Sources

Bulgur and tahini are available through the mail from Karnig Tashjian, 380 Third Avenue, New York, New York 10016 (212-683-8458). Ground cumin is available through the mail from H. Roth & Son, 1577 First Avenue, New York, New York 10028 (212-734-1110).

⏳ Köttbullar
Serves 8

(**SHOOT**-bool-lahr)

Meatballs are as popular in Sweden as hot dogs are in America. Unfortunately, most Americans have never tasted a decent Swedish meatball — the typical ersatz version is comparatively tasteless and usually heavy and overcooked.

I was introduced to true Swedish meatballs (*köttbullar*) in Skåne, the country's southernmost region. From this land, the warmest and most fertile in Sweden, come fruits, vegetables, cereal grains, and dairy products — as well as pork, beef, and veal, the three primary ingredients of *köttbullar*.

One of my hosts in Skåne served me *köttbullar* as an appetizer. He also initiated me into the "intoxicating" Swedish custom of skoaling. You raise a small glass of ice-cold aquavit chest high; while eyeing your friend, say "skoal." Next, you promptly throw the spirit down the hatch in one gulp and, if you're still up to it, look him once again squarely in the eye while giving a quick nod of camaraderie. You're now expected to quaff a glass of beer, the standard chaser.

½ cup unseasoned bread crumbs
½ cup half-and-half cream
4 tablespoons unsalted butter
¼ cup minced white onions
⅓ pound ground beef
⅓ pound ground veal
⅓ pound ground pork

1 large egg
⅛ teaspoon freshly grated
  nutmeg
½ teaspoon salt (or to taste)
¼ teaspoon freshly ground black
  pepper

Steps

1. Soak the bread crumbs in the half-and-half for 5 minutes in a large mixing bowl.
2. Melt 1 tablespoon of the butter in a small skillet over low to moderate heat. When the foam starts to subside, add the onions and sauté them for about 2 minutes. Let cool slightly.
3. Add the beef, veal, pork, egg, nutmeg, salt, pepper, and onions to the bread-crumb mixture. Gently combine the ingredients with your hands.

4. Cover the bowl and refrigerate the mixture for a couple of hours.
5. Shape the meat mixture with your hands into uniform ⅔-inch balls. Arrange them on a plate in one layer so they do not touch each other. Let the meatballs stand at room temperature for 30 minutes.
6. Melt the remaining butter in a sauté pan or skillet over moderate heat. When the foam starts to subside, add the meatballs. (Do not crowd the pan; unless your pan is oversized, you will have to cook the meatballs in batches and keep the cooked ones warm in a pre-heated 200° F oven.) Sauté the meatballs for about 5 minutes until they become brown on all sides. Turn them as necessary, but do so gently.
7. Transfer the *köttbullar* to a warm platter and serve immediately.

Additional Keys to Success

Don't overmix the ingredients in step 3 lest the meatballs become leaden. They should be light and succulent. ¶ Wetting your hands will help keep the meat from sticking to them in step 5.

Serving Suggestions and Affinities

Köttbullar of the size specified in this recipe make ideal hors d'oeuvres for cocktail parties. Serve them with toothpicks and, if you wish, a dipping sauce of your choice. ¶ Aquavit with a beer chaser is the traditional beverage.

Variations on a Theme

Köttbullar can be served at a smörgåsbord or as the main dinner entrée. In the latter case, shape the meat into 1- to 1¼-inch spheres and brown them briefly in a sauté pan. Then bake them, partially submerged in a cream-infused sauce, in a preheated 350° F oven for 30 minutes. Transfer the *köttbullar* to a warm bowl. Thicken the sauce with flour and pour it over the *köttbullar*. Popular accompaniments for this entrée include pickled beets, steamed or caramelized potatoes, and cucumber salad. ¶ *Köttbullar* can be made with one or two rather than three types of meat. ¶ Frugal Swedish cooks sometimes stretch their *köttbullar* with mashed leftover potatoes.

◦§ Mititei
(mih-tih-tay)

Serves 4 to 6

Rumanians are the most gregarious people of Eastern Europe. This vitality carries over into their eating preferences: They relish flavorful foods, especially *mititei.*

Mititei, which loosely translates as "extremely small," defines finger-sized, garlic-infused skinless sausages cooked on a grill over a bed of hot coals. They are easy to make and, as I discovered during my wanderings through Rumania, habit-forming. My addiction grew as I sampled them day in and day out — on a collective farm in the fertile Danube plain, at cafés along the sunny Black Sea coast, and on the bustling avenues of Bucharest, where street vendors do a land-office business. In all cases, the *mititei* were savory and succulent.

Rumanians eat *mititei* mainly as appetizers or between-meal snacks, sometimes accompanying them with a glass of *tuica* — the fiery Rumanian plum brandy. At other times the beverage is beer or one of Rumania's many sound table wines.

1 pound ground beef
¼ cup unseasoned beef stock
   (see page 195)
1 teaspoon finely chopped garlic
1 teaspoon salt (or to taste)
¼ teaspoon ground rosemary

½ teaspoon chopped fresh
   parsley
¼ teaspoon freshly ground black
   pepper
Pinch of cloves
Olive oil (for basting)

Steps

1. Put all the ingredients except the oil into a bowl. Mix them into a semismooth mass with your hands.
2. Cover the bowl and refrigerate overnight.
3. Remove the bowl from the refrigerator at least 1 hour before you proceed to step 4.
4. Roll the mixture by hand into uniform cylindrical sausages measuring approximately 3 inches long by 1 inch thick.
5. Place the sausages in a single, nontouching layer on a barbecue grate 3 inches above the hot coals (or on a lightly oiled grate in a pan 3 inches under a preheated 550° F oven broiler). Baste them

initially, and every 2 minutes thereafter. Turn them every 2 minutes. Cook the sausages until their exterior surfaces become crisp and brown, which should take a total of 6 to 8 minutes, depending on the intensity of the heat.

6. Transfer the cooked *mititei* to a heated dish and serve promptly.

Additional Keys to Success

Do not use lean ground beef. Fat adds flavor and helps keep the sausages from drying out during the barbecuing (or broiling) process. ¶ If you chop or grind the meat yourself, first remove any gristle. ¶ Combine and mold the *mititei* mixture more forcefully and compactly than you would hamburger patties. ¶ A 12- to 24-hour rest gives the ingredients in the mixture a chance to blend and generate new flavors. ¶ To keep the meat from sticking to your hands when shaping a sausage, moisten them with water. ¶ Turn the sausages with tongs, because piercing them with a fork or other penetrating instrument allows the succulent internal juices to escape. ¶ Don't overcook the sausages or the garlic will become bitter and the meat dry and tough.

Serving Suggestions and Affinities

Accompany the *mititei* with hot peppers in oil, sour pickles, sauerkraut, brynza (or feta) cheese, and crusty rye or pumpernickel bread. ¶ Uncork a robust red wine such as Premiat Cabernet Sauvignon, imported from Rumania. Beer, too, is a good partner for *mititei,* as is plum brandy.

Variations on a Theme

Substitute ground pork or lamb for the beef. ¶ Experiment with other herbs and spices. ¶ Adjust the garlic quantity to your taste. If you reduce the garlic content too much, though, you won't be cooking *mititei.*

Mail-Order Source

Rosemary is available through the mail from H. Roth & Son, 1577 First Avenue, New York, New York 10028 (212-734-1110).

⋖§ Mofongo   *Serves 4 to 6*
(moh-FOHN-go)

Most tourists to Puerto Rico explore San Juan but little else. Those who venture beyond the capital city usually seclude themselves within the confines of a large beach-resort hotel, thereby missing the opportunity of motoring through the incredibly beautiful countryside.

Except for the coastal plains that encircle the island, most of the Puerto Rican terrain is mountainous. When Queen Isabella asked Columbus, "What does your newly discovered island look like?" the navigator-explorer crushed a piece of paper in his fist and said, "Like this."

While driving through Puerto Rico's forest-clad tropical mountains, I visited a small farm where I was introduced to *mofongo,* the Puerto Rican meatball, consisting of deep-fried plantains and pork belly seasoned and mashed together into 1- to 3-inch spheres. "Some Puerto Rican cooks make *mofongo* so heavy you need a machete to split them," my host said, laughing. "Not so with my wife's recipe."

⅓ pound fresh pork belly
Vegetable oil (for deep-frying)
2 medium-sized plantains
1 teaspoon fresh lemon juice

¼ teaspoon finely minced garlic
¼ teaspoon salt (or to taste)
⅛ teaspoon freshly ground black
   pepper

Steps

1. Bring the pork belly to room temperature. Preheat the oven to 200° F.
2. Heat vegetable oil at least 3 inches deep to 370° F in a deep-fryer (or heavy-bottomed 3-quart saucepan).
3. Peel the plantains and slice them into ½-inch-thick segments. Cut the pork belly into ½-inch cubes.
4. Deep-fry the plantain rounds for roughly 5 minutes, or until they are light brown, turning the pieces occasionally. Transfer the plantain rounds to paper towels, pat them dry, and keep them warm in the oven.
5. Deep-fry the pork belly cubes for 5 minutes, or until they become crisp and light brown but not burnt, turning the pieces occasionally. Transfer them to paper towels and pat them dry.

6. Blend the plantains, pork belly, lemon juice, garlic, salt, and pepper in a food processor or electric blender. (Or perform the task in the old-fashioned but not necessarily better way: with a mortar and pestle.) The mixture should be the consistency of a coarse paste.

7. Shape the mixture into 1-inch balls. Serve promptly.

Additional Keys to Success

Use semiripe plantains. A plantain has reached this stage when approximately one quarter of the surface of its peel is covered with brownish-black spots. If you buy an unripe plantain, bring it to the semiripe stage by storing it for a day or two at room temperature in a paper bag that has had several holes pierced in it. ¶ Depending on the width of your deep-frying pan, you may have to cook the plantains and pork belly in batches. It is important not to crowd the pan. ¶ Because of their high fat content, *mofongo* lose their appeal as they lose their warmth.

Serving Suggestions and Affinities

Arrange the *mofongo* on a warm platter. Garnish with parsley sprigs. Provide toothpicks. ¶ Prepare a dipping sauce of your choice. For example: a mixture of ¼ cup freshly squeezed lemon juice, ½ teaspoon finely minced chili pepper, 2 tablespoons finely chopped coriander leaves, and ¼ teaspoon salt (or to taste).

Variations on a Theme

Fashion large *mofongo* balls — say, 2 inches in diameter. If you plan to serve them as the entrée for dinner, shape them 3 inches thick and crown them with a lemon-infused gravy. ¶ Pan-fry rather than deep-fry the plantains and pork belly in steps 4 and 5. ¶ Wrap a ¼-inch-thick layer of the *mofongo* mixture around a warm, peeled hard-cooked egg. ¶ Experiment by adding other flavoring agents in step 6.

✺ Mozzarella in Carrozza *Serves 8*
(MOHT-zah-REH-lah een kah-ROHT-zah)

"If God loves cheese sandwiches," a village priest in Italy proudly confided to me, "his favorite would be *mozzarella in carrozza.*" The padre was extolling a heavenly combination of crustless Italian bread and mozzarella, dipped in egg batter and then deep-fried until golden brown.

I first sampled *mozzarella in carrozza* (which translates as "mozzarella in a carriage") on a fall evening in a rustic home belonging to the owner of a small vineyard outside Naples. Everywhere the scent of fermenting grapes hung in the air, reminding me that winter was approaching. The warmth of the freshly made *mozzarella in carrozza* furnished a pleasant counterpoint to the light chill permeating the hilly countryside.

Rural kitchens are not the only source of *mozzarella in carrozza.* I've purchased more than my fair share of this treat from Neapolitan street vendors, enterprising souls who deep-fry their edibles in front of hungry passers-by. They do a brisk business, particularly when there is a breeze to waft the tantalizing aroma down the block.

Campania — Naples is the region's capital — is known for its hearty food. Specialties besides *mozzarella in carrozza* include pizza and various spaghetti dishes. Seafood, thanks to the bountiful coastline, is plentiful and worthy, as are tomatoes and eggplants. Seasonings include garlic and oregano. Olive oil, of course, is the region's frying medium.

Olive oil

1 thick loaf Italian (or French) bread

1 pound mozzarella

3 large eggs

2 tablespoons cream

¼ teaspoon salt (or to taste)

Steps

1. Pour olive oil into a heavy- and wide-bottomed pan to a depth of at least 2 inches. Heat the oil to 370° F.
2. Slice twenty-four ⅓-inch-thick slices from the center of the bread. Trim the crusts from the bread.
3. Slice the mozzarella into ¼-inch-thick ovals. The pieces of cheese should be slightly smaller than the bread slices.

4. Construct twelve sandwiches with the bread and cheese.

5. Put the eggs, cream, and salt into a shallow, flat-bottomed bowl. Beat the mixture.

6. Dip the sandwiches two or three at a time in the egg mixture. Let each side soak for 30 seconds. If the edges of the bread are dry, roll them in the egg mixture.

7. Seal the cheese inside each sandwich by lightly pressing together the edges of the two bread slices.

8. Deep-fry the sandwiches several at a time for approximately 1½ minutes per side, or until they are golden brown.

9. With a slotted spoon, transfer the fried sandwiches to paper towels. Pat them dry and serve immediately.

Additional Keys to Success

Deep-fry at (or within 5° F of) 370° F. If the temperature is too low, the bread will absorb too much oil. If the temperature is too high, the cheese will not have melted by the time the bread is golden brown. ¶ When a heated oil reaches its smoke point, it starts to decompose chemically and thereby develops negative cooking qualities. If you follow the popular "till a haze forms over the oil" guideline, you've already reached the smoke point. Therefore, use a deep-frying thermometer. ¶ Use only a high-quality olive oil, since most other olive oils have smoke points well below 370° F. If one is not available, use a high-quality corn, peanut, safflower, or sunflower oil. ¶ The cross section of the bread loaf should be approximately 2 inches high by 3 inches wide. ¶ For the sake of making the bread slices uniform, keep the adjacent slices together as you cut the bread. ¶ Do not overbeat the eggs in step 5. Otherwise, large bubbles will form and may burst, causing the oil to spatter in step 8.

Serving Suggestions

Mozzarella in carrozza can be eaten out of hand or with a knife and fork. ¶ This specialty must be served very hot, before the partially melted cheese solidifies.

Variations on a Theme

Coat the sandwiches with bread crumbs after step 7. ¶ Pan-fry rather than deep-fry the sandwiches. ¶ Ladle a tomato (or other) sauce over the *mozzarella in carrozza* just before serving. ¶ Experiment with other semisoft melting cheeses.

⋖§ Pierogi
(peer-o-gee)

Serves 4 to 6

Poland stretches from the sandy beaches of the Baltic Sea in the north to the snow-capped peaks of the Tatra Mountains in the south. The heartland of Poland comprises rolling hills and plains (Polska, the name Poles give to their country, means "plains").

These central lands are cultivated with fields of rye, barley, and potatoes and dotted with livestock. Pigs are important in Poland because ham is one of the nation's two best-known exports; vodka, which the Poles invented, is the other.

A large part of Poland is still undeveloped. Secluded rivers and lakes teeming with carp and pike and dense forests patrolled by wild boars and other beasts are quite common.

Poles are big on holidays, especially when the event furnishes an excuse to gather with family and friends to sing, dance, and feast. I once visited a small village outside Warsaw that was in the midst of a wedding. Just as I arrived, I saw the bride and groom, and the wedding party, leaving the wood-framed church. Most of the people were gaily outfitted in the traditional costumes, which for the women included leather boots, brightly colored skirts and bodices, and kerchiefs.

The wedding feast took place in the dirt road that split the village in half. The food was plentiful. My favorites were the *pierogi*, and the very best of them were prepared on top of a brick stove in a thatched cottage by the bride's grandmother. Here's her recipe for these half-moon-shaped miniturnovers.

4 tablespoons unsalted butter	Heaping ¼ teaspoon salt (or to taste)
¼ cup minced ham	
1 tablespoon chopped scallions	2 cups flour
1 cup cottage cheese	2 large eggs
1 tablespoon chopped fresh parsley	⅓ cup cold tap water
⅛ teaspoon freshly ground black pepper	1 tablespoon bread crumbs

Steps

1. Prepare the filling: Melt 1 tablespoon of the butter in a skillet over low to moderate heat. Sauté the ham and scallions for about 2 minutes. Let cool. Blend the ham-scallion mixture with the cottage cheese, parsley, pepper, and ¼ teaspoon of the salt in a bowl. Reserve for step 7.
2. Add approximately 3 quarts of water to a wide pot. Bring to a boil.
3. Put the flour in a mixing bowl. Form it into a mound and make a well in its center. Add the eggs, cold water, and remaining salt to the well. Blend the ingredients with a wooden spoon: Start in the center of the well and gradually work outward, using a circular motion. Knead the dough on a lightly floured board (or in the mixing bowl) for several minutes.
4. Cut the dough in half. On a lightly floured board, roll each half into a ⅛-inch-thick sheet.
5. Cut out 3-inch disks with a cookie cutter (or the rim of a glass).
6. Moisten the edge of each disk with water.
7. Place a rounded teaspoonful of the filling just off center on each disk. Fold each disk in half to cover the filling. Seal in the filling by crimping the circular edges of the *pierogi.*
8. With a slotted spoon, place one batch of *pierogi* in the boiling water. Don't crowd the pot.
9. As soon as the *pierogi* rise to the surface, they are cooked. Using the slotted spoon, immediately remove them from the water and transfer them to a warm plate.
10. Melt the remaining butter in a clean sauté pan or skillet over moderate heat. Add the bread crumbs and sauté them for about 30 seconds. Add a batch of the drained *pierogi.* Lightly brown them, for about 2 to 3 minutes per side.
11. Transfer the *pierogi* to a warm bowl and serve immediately.

Additional Keys to Success

The dough will stick less to your hands if you flour them lightly before kneading. ¶ To keep the dough from drying out and thereby not sealing properly, do not wait for more than 10 minutes between kneading the dough and rolling it out. ¶ For light *pierogi,* the dough must be rolled out thinly. ¶ The filling will ooze out unless the *pierogi* are securely sealed. ¶ If the *pierogi* are positioned too tightly in the pot, they will become gummy and may stick together. ¶ Do not crowd the sauté pan. Otherwise the *pierogi* will steam rather than brown.

Serving Suggestions

Pierogi can be served by themselves as an appetizer. They are also an excellent accompaniment to soup.

Variations on a Theme

Eliminate step 10, the browning process. ¶ *Pierogi* can be made with a yeast or soda dough, or with short pastry. ¶ The variety of fillings is limited only by the imagination of the cook. Popular fillings include savory chopped meat; a medley of mushrooms, rice, and onions; seasoned cooked cabbage; mashed potatoes; and fruits (when making dessert *pierogi*).

✑ Rillettes   *Serves 12 to 16*

(ree-YET)

The Loire — some six hundred miles long — is the longest river in France. After thrashing its way through mountain canyons in the Massif Central, the Loire slows down to a leisurely pace, carving a lazy S through gentle undulating hills graced by sixteenth-century Renaissance châteaux — the grand Chambord and the romantic Chenonceaux come quickly to mind.

The Loire Valley has been dubbed "The Garden of France" for good reason. The region's climate is ideal for growing foods because of the warm, moist air borne by the Gulf Stream. "It is the most precious gift your part of the world has given me," a local farmer told me.

As you drive down country lanes, you see commercial acreage abloom with flowers and orchards adorned with peaches and pears waiting to be picked and rushed by overnight truck to the markets of Paris. Less perishable produce sometimes reaches distant towns on a canal barge — the Loire is connected by manmade waterways to two of France's other great rivers, the Seine and the Rhône.

Vineyards are nearly everywhere. Among the many wines produced in the Loire Valley, Vouvray is the one most likely to be found in your neighborhood wine shop.

Carp, pike, and other freshwater piscatory delights swim in the Loire and its many tributaries. Populating the land are poultry, cattle, sheep, and — let's not forget — the pigs that make the potted meat specialty of the Loire Valley possible. I'm speaking of *rillettes*, a flavored spread that is usually made from pork fat and flesh.

2 pounds lean pork bellies
1 cup diced fatback
2 tablespoons water
1 teaspoon minced garlic
Heaping ½ teaspoon ground
    sage

1 small bay leaf
¼ teaspoon salt (or to taste)
¼ teaspoon freshly ground black
    pepper

Steps

1. Preheat the oven to 275° F.
2. Remove the rind and any bones from the pork bellies. Cut them into 1-inch cubes.
3. Place the fatback in a 3- to 4-quart casserole and partially render it for several minutes on top of the stove over moderate heat.
4. Add and stir in the cubed pork bellies. Add the water, garlic, sage, bay leaf, salt, and pepper. Stir the mixture well.
5. Place the casserole in the oven and bake for 2½ hours, turning the meat halfway through the cooking period.
6. Strain the preparation through a sieve over a stainless steel bowl. With the back of a wooden spoon, press out most of the juices from the meat. Discard the bay leaf. On a chopping board or in a small bowl, shred the meat, using two forks (at this stage, the meat should shred easily).
7. Put the meat in an earthenware crock or porcelain ramekin, packing it semifirmly.
8. Pour a ¼-inch layer of strained fat over the meat. If any pieces of shredded meat project upward to the top of the fat layer, press them down with the back of a spoon or fork.
9. Cover the container with a lid or aluminum foil and refrigerate it. Thus stored, the *rillettes* will stay fresh for at least a month. Serve at room temperature.

Additional Keys to Success

Buy pork belly that contains, at most, only a few small bones. ¶ Ask your butcher to remove the skin (it can be used to make pork cracklings). ¶ Do not substitute salt pork for the fatback. The latter, which comes from the back of the pig, has not been salted. ¶ In step 6, the meat should be shredded but not pulverized.

Serving Suggestions and Affinities

Bring the refrigerated *rillettes* to room temperature about 2 hours before serving it. Otherwise it will be too thick for easy spreading. ¶ Before serving, scrape off the top fat layer or, as some diners prefer, mix it with the lower layer. ¶ Spread the *rillettes* on slices of crusty French bread. ¶ Select a light-bodied red wine with relatively high acidity — a young Chinon or Beaujolais, for instance.

Variations on a Theme

Experiment with pork shoulder and other parts of the pig. ¶ Substitute goose meat and fat for the pork. ¶ Make *rillettes* with a combination of goose and pork. ¶ Prepare fattier *rillettes* by using a less lean piece of pork belly.

✑ Yalanci Dolma   *Serves 8 to 12*
(yuh-LAHN-jeh DOHL-mah)

Europe and Asia, in the vicinity of Istanbul, are separated by the Bosporus. This strait is among the busiest in the world: Jammed ferries crisscross it twenty-four hours a day and private yachts and goliath warships steadily pass through it, as if on parade. Going any which way are the fishing boats in search of the tasty bounty that may end up grilled that evening in one of the many hectic outdoor restaurants strung along the European shoreline.

The Asian, or Anatolian, side of the Bosporus pulses at a slower rate. Within a few minutes' drive from the ferry terminal, I was in the midst of fertile farms and blooming orchards.

On this exploratory trip I met a farmer's wife who had earned a stellar reputation in the nearby village for her *dolma*. This word means "stuffed." The filling can be almost anything — and the casing could be cabbage leaves or even a hollowed out cucumber, squash, or onion. Since the most celebrated combination is rice-stuffed vine leaves, *yalanci dolma*, I made sure that I learned how the farmer's wife prepared her version.

3 dozen vine leaves
¼ cup olive oil
⅔ cup chopped white onions
1 cup long-grain white rice
⅓ cup pine nuts
2 tablespoons chopped raisins
1 tablespoon crumbled dried mint

½ teaspoon ground dried oregano
½ teaspoon salt (or to taste)
Heaping ¼ teaspoon cinnamon
¼ teaspoon freshly ground black pepper
¼ cup fresh lemon juice
1½ cups boiling water

Steps

1. Prepare the vine leaves (see instructions below).
2. Heat the olive oil in a large sauté pan or skillet over low heat. Sauté the onions for 2 minutes, stirring frequently.
3. Add the rice. Stir the mixture frequently for 3 minutes.
4. Add the pine nuts, raisins, mint, oregano, and salt. Stir the mixture for 2 minutes. Then turn off the heat and wait several minutes before stirring in the cinnamon and pepper.
5. Construct the *dolma*, one by one, forming ⅔-by-2-inch cylinders: First, lay a leaf on the work surface, dull side up and with the stem end facing you. Place a rounded tablespoon of the rice mixture in the center of the leaf. Fashion this mixture into a horizontal (left-to-right) rectangular mound. Fold the stem end over the rice mixture. Next, fold over the sides of the leaf. Finish making the cylinder by rolling the package away from you. Expect to make about twenty *dolma*.
6. Line the bottom of a large, thick-, wide-, and flat-bottomed sauté (or other shallow, straight-sided) pan with a single layer of the unused vine leaves.
7. Place the *dolma* seam side down in the pan in neat, semitight rows.
8. Pour the lemon juice evenly over the *dolma*. Next, pour the 1½ cups of freshly boiled water over the *dolma*.

9. Weight the *dolma* down with a heavy, heat-proof, flat plate that just fits into the pan. This helps prevent the *dolma* from losing their symmetrical shape as they cook.

10. Bring the preparation to a simmer over low to moderate heat. Cover the pan and gently simmer the *dolma* for 35 to 40 minutes, or until the rice has absorbed most of the liquid.

11. Turn off the heat, remove the lid and plate, and let the preparation come to room temperature. The rice should absorb the excess liquid as it cools. If not, drain off the remaining liquid.

12. Serve chilled or at room temperature. In the former case, refrigerate the *dolma* for at least 1 hour. If you transfer the *dolma* from the pan to a serving platter, be careful not to rip the leaves.

Vine Leaf Preparation

Cut off the fibrous stems (if any) with a knife or scissors. Be careful not to rip the leaves.

If the leaves are fresh, thoroughly wash them in warm tap water. Soften these leaves by placing them a few at a time in a large pot of boiling water. As each leaf is parboiled for 2 to 3 minutes, drain it and place it on a flat surface, shiny side down. Keep the leaves separated.

If the leaves are brined, as are the ones sold in glass jars or out of a barrel, then gently rinse off as much of their excess salt as possible in two or more changes of hot tap water.

Additional Keys to Success

When using fresh vine leaves, select young and tender specimens. ❡ If you use brined vine leaves, reduce the salt quantity in the recipe by half (no matter how well you rinse these leaves, some salt will remain). ❡ Usually forty or more vine leaves are packed in a 12-ounce jar. Select the choicest (untorn) leaves for stuffing and save the rejects for lining the pan. ❡ If you add the cinnamon or pepper in step 4 before the pan has slightly cooled, those spices may scorch and therefore become bitter. ❡ In step 5, each *dolma* should be rolled in a reasonably tight but not taut bundle. You need to leave some room for the expansion of the rice as it cooks. ❡ Unless the *dolma* are packed snugly and seam side down, the rice may ooze out as it expands. ❡ If you have more *dolma* than can fit into a single layer in the pan, start a second layer. Fill up empty spaces with surplus vine leaves. ¶ In step 10, the water must simmer but not boil. The lid must not be removed until near the end of the cooking period or some of the needed steam will escape. ¶ Do not overcook the preparation in step 10. Otherwise the rice will become mushy.

Serving Suggestions and Affinities

Eat *dolma* with your fingers. ¶ Furnish each guest with a lemon wedge for squeezing over the *dolma.* ¶ *Dolma* can be enjoyed as an appetizer or as part of a salad plate. ¶ Since *yalanci dolma* can be made a day ahead of time, it is a convenient party dish.

Variations on a Theme

Dolma can be prepared in the oven. ¶ Experiment with other flavoring agents, such as garlic. ¶ Eliminate the pine nuts and/or raisins from the recipe. ¶ Substitute broth or tomato juice for the water in step 10. ¶ *Dolma* can be made with the addition of ground lamb. In this case the *dolma* are served hot, usually with a sauce. ¶ Some chefs completely cook the rice before they stuff the vine leaves. The chief drawback to this variation is that the rice inside the *dolma* won't expand, and therefore the *dolma* won't be as plump as they should be.

Leftovers

Cover the bowl or plate of *dolma* with plastic wrap and refrigerate the dish for up to several days. A *dolma* often improves in flavor as it sits in the refrigerator.

Mail-Order Source

Pine nuts and brined vine leaves are available through the mail from Karnig Tashjian, 380 Third Avenue, New York, New York 10016 (212-683-8458).

Soups ❧

✌§ Erwtensoep   *Serves 4 to 6*
(EHR-ton-soop)

"God made the world in seven days, but we made Holland in seven centuries," a barge captain proclaimed to me as he steered his wooden freight vessel through a rural canal spanned by many low-slung bridges. He explained that more than half the real estate now called Holland was once submerged. The enterprising Dutch needed space — Holland is the most densely populated nation in the world — so they set out to reclaim the land from the water.

Gradually, the land was rescued and protected from the incessant waves of the North Sea and the eroding flow of the rivers. Dikes, miles long and 10 to 30 feet high, were built. Windmills numbering ten thousand sprouted across the landscape to drain the ever-returning water. Today this chore is performed chiefly by electrical pumping stations.

From the deck of a barge I studied the reclaimed land passing before me. Holland's black and white dairy cattle nibbled grass from the pastures that surrounded small brick farmhouses warmly bedecked with potted flowers resting on windowsills — the Dutch adore the vibrant colors of nature.

There was a nip in the air on this early autumn day. *Erwtensoep* weather! The captain's wife prepared a steaming pot of this green pea soup for her live-aboard family and crew. Her soup was almost thick enough to support my spoon as I dipped it in for my first bite. I finished the bowl and asked for seconds. No wonder *erwtensoep* is considered the national soup of Holland.

1 pig's foot
6 cups water
3 cups (1½ pounds) dried split
peas
1 smoked ham hock
2 medium-sized boiling
potatoes, peeled and diced
½ cup sliced leeks
⅓ cup sliced white onions
3 tablespoons thinly sliced celery

1 teaspoon ground thyme
¼ teaspoon freshly grated
nutmeg
1 tablespoon fresh lemon juice
Heaping ½ teaspoon salt (or to
taste)
¼ teaspoon freshly ground black
pepper
½ pound cooked kielbasa

Steps

1. Bring to a boil enough water to parboil the pig's foot. Parboil it for 2 minutes. Drain and rinse it. Reserve it for step 3.

2. Bring the 6 cups of water to a boil in a 4- to 5-quart thick-bottomed pot.

3. Rinse the peas. Add them and the pig's foot and ham hock to the boiling water. Gently simmer the mixture, partially covered, for 2 hours. Stir occasionally.

4. Add all the remaining ingredients except the kielbasa and simmer gently, uncovered, for 30 minutes. Stir occasionally.

5. Remove the ham hock and pig's foot. Trim off their meat and return it to the pot.

6. Slice the kielbasa into ⅛-inch-thick rounds and add them to the pot.

7. Cook the soup for an additional 10 minutes; then serve it in a large tureen or individual bowls.

Additional Keys to Success

If you want to use uncooked kielbasa, add the slices to the soup in step 4. ¶ Substitute another firm smoked sausage if kielbasa is unavailable. If absolutely necessary, use smoked frankfurters. ¶ Some recipes specify a higher ratio of water to peas. Unless the soup is thick, however, it won't be authentic. ¶ Never let the soup boil.

Variations on a Theme

Substitute slab bacon for the kielbasa. Dice the bacon and add it in step 4. ❡ Instead of returning the cooked meat from the ham hock and pig's foot to the soup, serve it as a side dish. The diner spreads the meat on buttered pumpernickel or rye bread.

Leftovers

Erwtensoep improves each time it is stored and reheated, so plan to make a surplus quantity. You will probably have to perk up its seasonings, though.

Mail-Order Source

Kielbasa is available through the mail from Schaller and Weber, 1654 Second Avenue, New York, New York 10028 (212-879-3047).

❧ Harira   *Serves 4 to 6*
(hah-REE-rah)

Faithful Muslims fast from sunrise to sunset during the holy month of Ramadan. This abstention is particularly trying in countries such as Algeria when Ramadan happens to occur during the hot summer months (the Moslem year is based on 354 days, so the lunar Ramadan month drifts through the seasons over the course of several decades).

Ramadan hits the farmers worst of all. I've seen them toiling under the scorching Algerian sun without a drop of water passing their parched throats. By late afternoon, hunger also begins to take its toll.

The end of the day's fast (up to fifteen hours on the summer solstice) is signaled in towns and villages by cannon fire or by a chant from the top of a minaret. Farmers are forced to make their own calculations, perhaps by waiting until their eyes "can no longer distinguish a black from a white thread" in the natural light.

Traditionally, the edge of hunger and thirst is abated with a steaming bowl of the thick, curdled soup called *harira*. I've sampled many versions; this one is worth making any time of the year, regardless of whether you follow the dictums of the Koran.

1 lamb shank (1 to 1¼ pounds)
¼ cup fresh lemon juice
3 tablespoons olive oil
⅔ cup chopped white onions
1 teaspoon minced garlic
1 tablespoon minced fresh
   ginger
⅓ cup diced carrots
½ cup chopped ripe tomatoes
2 quarts water
1 medium-sized bay leaf
1½ tablespoons crushed dried
   mint

¼ teaspoon freshly grated
   nutmeg
Pinch of cloves
1 scant teaspoon salt (or to taste)
¼ teaspoon freshly ground black
   pepper
½ cup lentils
½ cup orzo
3 large eggs
1 tablespoon chopped fresh
   parsley

Steps

1. Marinate the lamb shank in the lemon juice for at least 12 hours in the refrigerator. Turn the meat occasionally.

2. Heat the oil in a 4- to 6-quart thick-bottomed pan over low heat. Sauté the onions for 2 minutes, stirring frequently. Add the garlic, ginger, and carrots and cook the mixture for 2 minutes, stirring frequently.

3. Stir in the tomatoes. Bring the mixture to a simmer and cook it for 5 minutes, stirring occasionally.

4. Add the lamb and its marinade as well as the water, bay leaf, mint, nutmeg, cloves, salt, and pepper. Stir well. Bring the liquid to a simmer. Cover the pot and gently simmer for 1½ hours, stirring occasionally.

5. Transfer the lamb to a warm plate and cover it with foil.

6. Discard the bay leaf. Stir the lentils into the pot and simmer, covered, for 20 minutes.

7. When the lamb is cool enough to handle, shred the meat and return it to the pot. Discard the bone and trimmings.

8. Stir the orzo into the broth when step 6 is completed. Simmer the mixture, covered, for 12 minutes.

9. Beat the eggs and stir them into the soup. The *harira* is done as soon as the eggs curdle (yes, curdling is called for). Serve the soup in individual bowls and sprinkle with parsley.

Additional Keys to Success

Trim off as much of the surface fat from the lamb shank as possible before you marinate it. ¶ If fresh, vine-ripened tomatoes are unavailable, use a top-quality Italian brand of plum tomatoes; be sure to drain them first. ¶ If the liquid boils while the lamb is in the pot, the meat will toughen unnecessarily. ¶ Before you cook the lentils, search for and discard any foreign matter such as small stones.

Serving Suggestions and Affinities

Harira can be served as the soup course. Or it can be the main course of a light lunch when accompanied by pita bread and dried fruits.

Variations on a Theme

Use cubed boneless lamb. In this case, add a lamb soup bone to the pot. ¶ Substitute chicken or kid for the lamb. ¶ In place of orzo, use *couscous,* rice, or a small pasta such as tubettini, stellini, anellini, acini di pepe, or semi de melone.

Mail-Order Sources

Fresh ginger, dried mint, and nutmeg are available through the mail from H. Roth & Son, 1577 First Avenue, New York, New York 10028 (212-734-1110). Orzo is available from Todaro Brothers, 555 Second Avenue, New York, New York 10016 (212-532-0633).

≈§ Scotch Broth   *Serves 4 to 6*

My last visit to the Scottish Highlands was in late summer. The low heather shrubs on the rocks and treeless wasteland had, within the past fortnight, exploded the desolate moorscape into a profusion of majestic purple.

   Scottish Blackface sheep, a breed well suited for the raw, cold winters of the Highlands, grazed in nearby narrow glens and open straths, and on the grassy shorelines of secluded blue lochs carved by prehistoric glaciers. I saw shepherds shearing some of their flock to obtain wool for thick sweaters and other clothing. Outerwear is needed in the cool of the approaching evening at this time of year in the Highlands. Without it, I would have shivered.

A few of the animals were slaughtered for their meat. When a cook makes a soup of mutton or lamb with barley harvested in the Central Lowlands, she has Scotch broth, the perfect nourishment for the hard-working family of a shepherd assembled around their spacious dining table. Being frugal, many Scots make barley broth (the local name for this soup) with the head of the sheep. This portion of the animal furnishes extra flavor and thickening power. Occasionally, the source of meat is deer that still flourish in the unsettled areas of the southern boundary of the Highlands, the Grampian Hills.

Another gastronomic miracle of the Highlands is whisky, spelled without the letter *e* in this part of the British Isles. Most Scots drink their whisky straight, and unlike nearly all the Scotch Whisky specimens that reach our country, their firewater is unblended with flavor-sapping neutral grain spirits. For anyone who has never tasted the real McCoy, I suggest sipping or bolting a jigger of one of the single malt whiskies such as The Glenlivet and Glenfiddich. They have sufficient verve and complexity to make you hear "Scotland the Brave" being played by a small army of bagpipers dressed in colorful plaid kilts.

2 pounds bone-in lamb shoulder	½ cup medium pearl barley
2 quarts cold water	¼ cup chopped white onions
2 teaspoons vinegar	½ cup coarsely chopped leeks
Heaping ½ teaspoon salt (or to taste)	¼ cup finely diced carrots
¼ teaspoon freshly ground black pepper	¼ cup finely diced turnips
	1 tablespoon chopped fresh parsley

Steps

1. Trim off and discard the exterior lamb fat.
2. Put the lamb, cold water, vinegar, salt, and pepper into a 4-quart pot.
3. Bring the liquid to a boil; immediately reduce the heat to low. Simmer the soup, uncovered, for 45 minutes. Skim off the scum as it accumulates.

4. Stir in all the remaining ingredients except the parsley. Cover and simmer the soup for 45 minutes.

5. Remove the lamb. When it is cool enough to handle, shred the meat and return it to the pot (discard the bones and trimmings).

6. Stir the soup and ladle it into warm bowls. Garnish each bowl with chopped parsley.

Additional Keys to Success

You can substitute neck or shank for the lamb shoulder. The neck produces a thicker broth; the shank yields more meat. ¶ If you use cut-up lamb pieces, reduce the initial cooking stage by 10 to 15 minutes. ¶ The meat will toughen unnecessarily if you cook above a low simmer.

Variations on a Theme

Many peasant homes serve this dish in two separate courses: The broth (either strained or with the vegetables) precedes the meat. In this case, the meat is cut into cubes rather than shredded. ¶ In Scotland the dish is made as often with mutton as it is with lamb. When using mutton, add 30 minutes to the first cooking stage. ¶ Cabbage, celery, parsnips, peas, and rutabagas are among the other vegetables that are sometimes incorporated into the dish. ¶ Some recipes call for herbs such as bay leaf and cinnamon, but herbs and spices do not play an important role in Scottish peasant cuisine.

Affinities

Crusty bread goes well with Scotch broth. Complementary side dishes include steamed or boiled potatoes as well as kale or other green vegetables.

Mail-Order Source

Pearl barley is available through the mail from H. Roth & Son, 1577 First Avenue, New York, New York 10028 (212-734-1110).

✍ Sopa de Ajo   *Serves 4*
(soh-pah deh ah-hoh)

Near a whitewashed house in a quiet village of La Mancha sat a quintet of children, all clearly under five and bored with the midafternoon inactivity of hamlet life. With nothing else to do, they divided their attention between me and a hawker, who deftly poured his product from a large earthenware vessel into a smaller one without losing a single drop. He was selling me virgin olive oil, which I would use that evening for making *sopa de ajo,* garlic soup.

The fruit for the oil grew in the high tableland of central Spain, an austere region that would be virtually treeless were it not for the olive groves. La Mancha also has vineyards, vast fields of corn waving in the breeze, and dusty open fields treaded upon by sheep languorously moving forward, searching for precious blades of grass. "In the summer it is too hot; in the winter, too cold," a shepherd with a weather-wrinkled face complained to me. La Mancha is a land of climatic extremes.

It is also the setting for Cervantes's famous novel *Don Quixote de La Mancha,* in which the wandering knight-errant roams the world with rusty lance, puny nag, and true-blue friend Sancho Panza in an effort to right the wrongs of the world and win the heart of Dulcinea.

1 quart water	¼ teaspoon ground red pepper
4 slices slightly stale white bread	(cayenne)
¼ cup olive oil	½ teaspoon salt (or to taste)
2 tablespoons minced garlic	

Steps
1. Boil the water.
2. Trim the crust off the bread. Cut the slices into ½-inch cubes.
3. Heat the olive oil in a wide- and heavy-bottomed 2- to 3-quart pot over low heat.
4. Fry the garlic for 15 seconds, stirring constantly.
5. Add the bread, raise the heat to low to moderate, and sauté the bread for 3 to 5 minutes, until the cubes are lightly brown. Stir constantly.

6. Add the boiling water, cayenne, and salt. Simmer uncovered for 12 minutes, stirring occasionally. Serve immediately.

Additional Keys to Success

If you don't have slightly stale bread, place cubes made from fresh bread slices on a plate and let stand uncovered at room temperature for at least 12 hours. Alternatively, place the fresh cubes on a cookie sheet in the middle of a preheated 200° F oven for 15 to 20 minutes. ¶ If the temperature of the oil is too high in steps 4 and 5, the garlic will burn and become bitter. ¶ The fragrant scent of a rich olive oil is characteristic of this soup, so use a high-quality, imported virgin olive oil if available.

Serving Suggestions and Affinities

For a traditional touch, ladle *sopa de ajo* into earthenware bowls. ¶ For a light supper, serve *sopa de ajo* with a salad and crusty bread.

Variations on a Theme

For a richer soup, substitute chicken, veal, or fish stock for the water. ¶ Incorporate into the soup one or more of the following ingredients: diced tomatoes, diced green pepper, minced chorizo sausages, sweet paprika, lemon juice. ¶ Garnish the soup with chopped coriander leaves. ¶ Add two beaten eggs to the soup 1 minute before the end of step 6. ¶ Rather than adding beaten eggs, poach one egg per serving in the cooking soup. ¶ You can reduce the amount of garlic to suit your taste, but if you decrease it by too much, you won't be cooking authentic *sopa de ajo*.

Mail-Order Source

Chorizo sausages and sweet paprika are available through the mail from Casa Moneo Spanish Imports, 210 West 14th Street, New York, New York 10011 (212-929-1644).

✑ Soupa Avgolemono   *Serves 4*
(soo-pah ahv-goh-LEH-moh-noh)

My companion and I had just finished a pleasant midday meal at an
outdoor *taverna* strategically situated on the bay in Lindos, a small
village on the Greek island of Rhodes. We were supposed to catch
a boat in the town of Rhodes, on the northern tip of the island,
but decided to prolong our stay in Lindos a little longer because
we could not tear ourselves away from the beautiful setting. Above
us, on a promontory jutting into the Mediterranean Sea, loomed the
majestic ruins of the ancient acropolis of Rhodes. "If we miss the
boat, we miss the boat," we jointly rationalized.

Two hours and one bottle of retsina later, we hopped into our
rented sports car and headed down a road lined with shady hibiscus
trees, hoping to be in the town of Rhodes within ninety minutes.

Our plans were shelved when we were waylaid in the most pleasant of circumstances. We were passing through one of many rural
villages when — suddenly — scores of merrymakers began to cross
our route.

I stepped on the brakes, and before we knew it my friend and
I were politely but firmly pulled from the seats of our car. The gregarious citizens were insisting that we join in the wedding feast. As is
the custom in this village, the wedding party went to one home for
food and drink, then moved across the road to another dwelling,
and then on to other abodes until every relative had an opportunity
to play the role of host.

·Since we had recently finished a reasonably large lunch, we were
not hungry — or so we thought. All it took to rekindle our appetites
was a bowl of *soupa avgolemono*.

Avgolemono literally means "egg-lemon." The protein in the egg
gives the chicken broth a milky hue and the lemon juice offers a
tangy background note. Texture is contributed by the rice.

4 large eggs
6 cups unseasoned chicken stock
   (see page 195)
½ cup long-grain white rice

½ heaping teaspoon salt (or to
   taste)
¼ teaspoon freshly ground black
   pepper
¼ cup fresh lemon juice

Steps

1. Bring the eggs to room temperature. Bring the chicken stock to a boil. Stir in the rice, salt, and pepper and simmer the mixture for 15 minutes.

2. Beat the eggs rapidly and thoroughly until frothy. Beat the lemon juice, a tablespoon at a time, into the eggs. Beat 1 tablespoon, then 2 tablespoons, and then 4 tablespoons of the hot stock into the egg-lemon sauce.

3. Turn off the heat under the simmering stock. Slowly pour the egg-lemon sauce into the pan, stirring all the while. Keep stirring for 2 minutes or until the soup begins to thicken slightly. Serve immediately.

Additional Keys to Success

For the sake of texture, do not overcook the rice. ¶ Unless the eggs are well beaten in step 2, the egg whites may not blend thoroughly into the soup. ¶ The heating of the egg-lemon sauce in step 2 is necessary to prevent the eggs from curdling. ¶ If you forget to turn off the heat in step 3, the eggs are likely to curdle.

Serving Suggestions and Affinities

Serve *soupa avgolemono* by itself as a soup course. When it is accompanied by a basket of crusty bread, it can be the main course for a light lunch. ¶ Beverages generally don't go with *soupa avgolemono*.

Variations on a Theme

Prepare *soupa avgolemono* with lamb, beef, veal, or fish stock. ¶ Add meat slivers or minimeatballs to the soup. ¶ Substitute orzo or other tiny pasta for the rice. ¶ Use only the yolks of the eggs. ¶ Separate the eggs. Beat the egg whites to the soft-peak stage. Beat the yolks into the soup and then fold in the egg whites.

Leftovers

When reheating leftovers, warm the soup over low heat and stir frequently. The soup will probably curdle if it boils.

Mail-Order Source

Orzo is available through the mail from Karnig Tashjian, 380 Third Avenue, New York, New York 10016 (212-683-8458).

⮜§ Tarator   *Serves 4*
(tahr-ah-TOHR)

Bulgaria's eastern and northern borders are, respectively, the so-called Black Sea and blue Danube. I use the qualifier *so-called* because these two bodies of water are ineptly described. Unless I'm colorblind, the Black Sea is blue and the Danube muddy brown. Unlike the river, however, the green Danubian plain in the spring is aesthetically pleasing.

While visiting this region of Bulgaria, I took a side road to see a small vineyard. On the way I spotted a dozen farm workers taking lunch alongside a field of sugar beets. They invited me to join them, and I did. They handed me a wooden spoon and an enamelware bowl half-filled with a cold yogurt and cucumber soup called *tarator*. The soup was refreshing in the heat of the day, and the bowl, with its painted floral motif, was delightfully folksy.

Bulgarians are known for their enviable longevity — many a citizen lives to the ripe age of one hundred, I'm told. While it is poppycock that the secret of their good fortune lies in the large quantities of yogurt Bulgarians consume, this cultured dairy product probably plays at least some small role in helping them outlive their counterparts in other countries.

Don't get me wrong. I'm not suggesting that this recipe will add a few years to your lifetime. I do guarantee, though, that a little *tarator* now and then should make your days on earth a little more enjoyable.

3 small cucumbers	½ teaspoon salt (or to taste)
3 cups plain yogurt	5 tablespoons chopped walnuts
2 tablespoons olive oil	1 tablespoon chopped fresh dill
2 teaspoons finely minced garlic	

Steps

1. Peel the cucumbers. Slice them in half lengthwise. Scoop out and discard the seedy core. Cut the flesh into ¼-inch cubes.
2. Place the yogurt in a glass, stainless steel, or other noncorrosible bowl. Beat the yogurt for 1 minute with a spoon.
3. Beat in the olive oil 1 teaspoon at a time. Be sure each new teaspoon of the oil is thoroughly beaten into the yogurt before adding the next teaspoon.
4. Add the cucumber, garlic, salt, and all but 1 tablespoon of the walnuts to the bowl. Thoroughly blend the ingredients.
5. Cover the bowl and refrigerate the *tarator* and four individual soup bowls for at least 1 hour.
6. Remove the *tarator* from the refrigerator and neatly ladle it into the soup bowls. Garnish the top of each serving with dill and the remaining walnuts. Serve immediately.

Additional Keys to Success

Buy cucumbers that are small for their variety. Large cucumbers will be exceedingly seedy and their flavor will be too bitter (even soaking them in salted water won't completely diminish their bitter note). ¶ Whole-milk yogurt is preferable to the skimmed product. ¶ You can decrease the quantity of minced garlic to taste, but if you use less than 1 teaspoon, you shouldn't call your soup *tarator*. ¶ For the sake of color contrast, use nonwhite soup bowls. A deep red, black, or yellow hue is ideal. ¶ If fresh dill is unavailable, substitute fresh mint or, if necessary, fresh chives or parsley.

◂§ Tom Yam Kung   *Serves 6*
(tom yum koo'ng)

On a pole stuck into the ground in front of a farmhouse that I visited in Thailand was a miniature dwelling no larger than a rural mailbox. It looked like Walt Disney's version of a Siamese dollhouse, extravagantly decorated and floridly painted.

Standing next to this architectural spectacle was my hostess, a woman of classical Thai features: large and bright eyes, long black hair, golden brown skin. She was clad in a colorful, ankle-length silk dress called a *panyung*, which was tightly wrapped around her hips. Like most of the Thais I met, she had a calm and cheerful personality.

"You're looking at a spirit house," she informed me. "Nearly everyone constructs one of them near the entrance to their home to appease the land spirits. We periodically leave offerings in them, including small bouquets of flowers and steamed rice rolled in banana leaves.

"We don't feed our guests in our spirit houses." She laughed. "Besides, you're too big; so we'll eat inside my home." She served me and her family a variety of dishes plus rice, the starch staple of Thailand. All of us ate in the traditional Thai manner: with our fingers. A spoon, however, was provided for the *tom yam kung,* the leading soup of Thailand. This spicy shrimp soup gains its unique flavor from the stalk of the lemon grass plant and the leaves of the *makrut* lime tree.

1½ quarts water
1 pound unshelled small shrimp
3 tablespoons *nam pla* (or similar fish sauce)
1½ tablespoons shredded dried lemon grass

5 *makrut* (or *kaffir*) lime leaves
¼ cup thinly sliced scallions
¼ cup whole coriander leaves
2 tablespoons thinly sliced fresh green chili peppers

Steps

1. Boil the water in a 3- to 4-quart pot.
2. Shell and devein the shrimp. Add the shells along with the *nam pla,* lemon grass, and *makrut* leaves to the boiling water. Add all but approximately one fourth of the scallions, coriander leaves, and chili peppers to the boiling water.
3. Boil the mixture for 15 minutes.
4. Strain the mixture into another pot and bring the liquid to a simmer.
5. Stir in the shrimp and the uncooked scallions, coriander leaves, and chili peppers. Simmer for 2 to 3 minutes, depending on the thickness of the shrimp.
6. Ladle the *tom yam kung* into a warm tureen or into warm individual bowls.

Additional Keys to Success

If you can purchase them, substitute small prawns (with claws) for the shrimp. They are generally more flavorful. ¶ Try to purchase the crustaceans with their heads still attached. Boil the flavor-giving heads along with the shells in step 3. ¶ The best of the widely available substitutes for *nam pla* is *patis*, a Philippine fish sauce. ¶ There is no recommendable substitute for lemon grass. Some recipes call for lemon or lime juice, but without the unique flavor of lemon grass, the soup substantially changes character. ¶ Do not touch your eyes when you are slicing the chilies. As soon as you complete the cutting task, thoroughly wash your hands and the work surface. ¶ Shrimp cook quickly. Remember, they can irrevocably toughen as a result of cooking them for an extra minute or two.

Serving Suggestions and Affinities

Serve *tom yam kung* as a separate fish course or, as the Thais do, as part of a single course comprising a number of other dishes including plain rice. ¶ Don't accompany *tom yam kung* with a beverage if you serve the soup as a separate course.

Variations on a Theme

Sauté the shells in a little oil before adding them to the boiling water in step 2. ¶ Prepare *tom yam kung* with an unseasoned stock made from fish, chicken, or pork bones. ¶ Substitute chicken for the shrimp. (In this case, use an unseasoned chicken stock.) ¶ Add garnishes such as thinly sliced mushrooms. ¶ Some cooks serve the soup with the shredded lemon grass. This garnish should not be eaten, however, because the shreds are extremely fibrous.

Mail-Order Source

Nam pla, dried lemon grass, and *makrut* (*kaffir*) lime leaves are available through the mail from the Lynwood Market, 11325 Atlantic Avenue, Lynwood, California 90262 (213-635-9457).

Main
Dishes

✑ Adobo   *Serves 4*
(ah-DOH-boh)

Adobo, the national dish of the Philippines, has Mexican roots. The underlying concept of the preserving and cooking technique for *adobo* was introduced by some of the early Spaniards who had briefly settled in Mexico before moving to the Philippine Islands.

It didn't take long for Filipinos to fashion from this imported technique a dish that they could call their own. *Adobo* features four pillars of Philippine peasant cookery: It is sour, salty (thanks to the soy sauce), and garlic-infused, and it contains a combination of meats.

Adobo rapidly grew in popularity, especially on the main island of Luzon, because it was both tasty and practical. The acidity of the marinade serves a special function for Filipino peasants, who live in a hot climate without means of refrigeration. The *adobo*-making process allows them to preserve meat for several days before and after it is cooked.

Whenever I tasted *adobo* in the Philippines, it was served with rice, the starch staple of the islands. Some of the rice I ate was grown on the several-thousand-year-old Banaue rice terraces, which many a proud Filipino calls with justification the "Eighth Wonder of the World." These spectacular multitiered paddies are carved in curving parallel rows out of steep mountain slopes. If you could lay them end to end, they would stretch more than halfway around the world.

1 pound boneless lean pork loin
4 medium-sized chicken legs
½ cup rice vinegar
¼ cup water
3 tablespoons soy sauce

1 bay leaf
6 black peppercorns
3 cloves garlic
¼ cup vegetable oil

Steps

1. Cut the pork into 1½-inch cubes. Trim off and discard the exterior fat and gristle.
2. Divide each chicken leg into thigh and drumstick sections.
3. Put all the ingredients except the oil in a glass or other noncorrosible bowl. Mix all the ingredients well.
4. Cover the bowl and refrigerate the marinating meat for two days, turning the meat pieces occasionally.
5. Transfer the meat and its marinade to a heavy-bottomed 3- to 4-quart pot. Bring the liquid to a simmer. Reduce the heat, cover the pot, and gently simmer the preparation for 40 minutes, turning the pieces once.
6. Transfer the meat pieces with a slotted spoon to paper towels and pat them dry. Discard the bay leaf.
7. Reduce and thicken the sauce in the pan by increasing the heat and boiling the contents for 5 to 10 minutes, or until the sauce drips slowly from a spoon. Stir the mixture frequently.
8. Heat the oil in a large sauté pan or skillet over moderate heat (start this step immediately after you begin step 7). Add the meat and brown the pieces on all sides. Transfer them to a warm plate as you cook each batch.
9. Return the meat pieces to the pot and coat them on all sides with the reduced and thickened sauce. Serve the meat and its sauce immediately.

Additional Keys to Success

Substitute a good white wine vinegar for the rice vinegar if the latter is unavailable. ¶ Do not let the liquid boil in step 5 or the chicken and pork will toughen. If your gas burner cannot be adjusted to a very low setting, use a heat diffuser.

Serving Suggestions and Affinities

Plain white rice is the traditional accompaniment. You can serve the rice on the side or as a bed for your *adobo*. ¶ *Adobo* is too sour and salty for wine. Beer does the dish more justice.

Variations on a Theme

For a more flavorful meat, use the flesh from older chickens and pigs. If you do, extend the cooking time in step 5. ¶ *Adobo* can be made with chicken only, or with pork only. It can also be prepared with other meats. ¶ Substitute lime juice for some of the vinegar. ¶ Eliminate the water in step 3 and add ¼ cup of coconut cream before you start cooking the preparation in step 5. ¶ Add 1 to 2 tablespoons of shredded coconut to the preparation in step 9. ¶ Serve as a table condiment the Philippine seafood paste called *bagoong.*

Mail-Order Sources

Rice vinegar and coconut cream are available through the mail from Katagiri & Company, 224 East 59th Street, New York, New York 10022 (212-755-3566). Black peppercorns are available from H. Roth & Son, 1577 First Avenue, New York, New York 10028 (212-734-1110).

৺ **Arroz con Pollo**   *Serves 4*
(ah-ROHTH kohn POH-yoh)

Paella à la Valenciana, as the world knows it, is seldom eaten by Valencian peasants. Chefs in fancy restaurants from New York to Madrid too often make the dish ridiculously complex by incorporating into it everything in their larder: chicken, fish, lobster, shrimp, clams, mussels, what have you. While these big production numbers may dazzle the eye, they tend to overwhelm the palate.

The peasants, in contrast to their big-city cousins, prefer to use one or at most two meats in this Valencian specialty. Along the region's balmy Mediterranean coast, the star ingredient is most apt to be a shellfish, perhaps mussels or shrimp. Inland, when the littoral plain gives way to foothills and mountains, the cook's first choice is generally chicken — and, if this be the case, the dish is usually called *arroz con pollo* ("rice with chicken") rather than *paella.* A well-made, peasant-style *arroz con pollo* is infinitely superior to the run-of-the-mill restaurant-style *paella à la Valenciana* and is just as delicious as a great one. It's also quicker, easier, and less expensive to prepare.

Rice — the foundation of any *paella* or *arroz con pollo* — is a major crop in Valencia. This cereal grain was introduced to the Spanish Mediterranean coast two thousand years ago by Middle Eastern traders. These seafarers also brought with them what would turn out to be Valencia's most famous product, the orange. "On nights when orange blossoms open, the countryside is filled with a heady fragrance," the daughter of a Valencian farmer told me. "It's the aphrodisiac of Valencia."

3 pounds chicken drumsticks and thighs
2½ cups water
½ cup dry white wine
¾ teaspoon salt (or to taste)
1 bay leaf
4 tablespoons olive oil
1½ cups long-grain white rice

¾ cup chopped white onions
½ cup diced Italian sweet pepper
1 tablespoon minced garlic
½ cup diced tomatoes
1 tablespoon fresh lemon juice
½ teaspoon crushed saffron
2 tablespoons chopped fresh parsley

Steps

1. Remove the chicken from the refrigerator 45 minutes before beginning step 2.
2. Bring the water and wine to a boil in a 3- to 4-quart saucepan.
3. Add to the liquid the salt, bay leaf, and chicken drumsticks. Bring the mixture to a simmer. Cover the pot and gently simmer for 3 minutes.
4. Add the chicken thighs. Bring the mixture to a simmer. Cover and gently simmer for 10 minutes, turning the pieces after 5 minutes.
5. Transfer the chicken with a slotted spoon to several layers of paper towels and pat dry. Reserve the stock in the pan over low heat.
6. Heat the oil in a shallow casserole measuring at least 12 inches in diameter (or in a *paella* pan).
7. Brown the chicken pieces on all sides in the hot oil over moderate heat. (Brown in batches if necessary.)
8. Transfer the chicken to a warm bowl and cover it.
9. Add the rice to the casserole. Sauté it for 5 minutes, stirring frequently.

10. Reduce the heat to low to moderate. Add the onions and sauté them for 2 minutes. Add the Italian pepper and the garlic and sauté them for 1 minute. Stir constantly.
11. Add the tomatoes and lemon juice. Stir the mixture.
12. Strain the reserved chicken stock and add 2 cups of it to the casserole.
13. Add the saffron. Stir the mixture for 1 minute.
14. Arrange the chicken pieces on top of the rice. Bring the liquid to a simmer. Cover the pot and gently simmer for 15 to 20 minutes, until the rice has absorbed all the liquid.
15. Let the covered pot stand off the heat for 5 minutes.
16. Sprinkle the *arroz con pollo* with the parsley. Serve it at the table from the casserole.

Additional Keys to Success

Select thighs and drumsticks from a small to medium-sized chicken. ¶ Unless you proceed promptly from step 10 to step 11, your garlic will burn and become bitter. ¶ Use low heat in step 14 to avoid scorching the pot. ¶ Preserve steam in the pot by not lifting the lid during the cooking process in step 14.

Affinities

Serve beer or a young, dry medium-bodied white or light-bodied red wine.

Variations on a Theme

Use chicken breasts exclusively, or use them in combination with the thighs and drumsticks. ¶ Add diced chorizo or ham with the onions in step 10. ¶ Add green vegetables such as peas. ¶ Substitute rabbit or shellfish (lobster, shrimp, mussels, and clams are popular choices) for the chicken. Or combine a medley of these meats for a *paella*.

Mail-Order Source

Saffron is available through the mail from H. Roth & Son, 1577 First Avenue, New York, New York 10028 (212-734-1110).

⋖§ Bacalao a la Vizcaína   *Serves 4*
(bah-kah-LAH-oh ah lah veeth-kah-EE-nah)

The Basques are a fiercely independent people. Though their homeland lies partly in Spain and partly in France, they think of themselves
as being Basque, not Spanish or French. Good for them. They have
reason to be proud of their heritage because they have retained their
ethnic identity longer than any other European people. Some anthropologists trace their roots in the Pyrenees back to the end of the
Paleolithic period, some fifteen thousand years ago.

Despite the availability of fish freshly caught in the Bay of Biscay,
and the obvious fondness of the Basque for this seafood, the people
hold a special affection for *bacalao,* cod preserved with salt. Wherever
I traveled in the Basque province of Vizcaya, be it in small fishing
villages or in the hilly back country where the legendary Basque shepherds tend their flocks, I could smell the aroma of salt cod in the
pot.

More often than not, the salt cod preparation that my nose (and
sometimes my palate) detected was *bacalao a la vizcaína.* When salt
cod is simmered with such distinct ingredients as onions, garlic, lemon
juice, tomatoes, and wine, a wonderful flavor develops. The fact that
this specialty is superb shouldn't be a surprise because the Basques
are known in gourmet circles as being among the finest cooks in
Europe.

1½ pounds salt cod
4 tablespoons olive oil
1 cup sliced yellow onions
2 teaspoons minced garlic
½ cup dry white wine
1 cup chopped tomatoes
½ cup sliced Italian sweet
   pepper

1 tablespoon fresh lemon juice
1 teaspoon dried crushed mint
¼ teaspoon ground red pepper
   (cayenne)
4 lemon slices
1 tablespoon chopped fresh
   parsley

Steps

1. Cover the cod with cold tap water in a stainless steel pot or glass
bowl. Soak the fish at room temperature for 15 to 18 hours, changing
the water at least twice.

2. Cut the cod into thick, 1½-inch-square segments. Carefully transfer the pieces to a 3- to 4-quart saucepan. Cover the cod with cold water. Bring the liquid to a boil and gently simmer for 10 minutes. (Note: As you are working on steps 2 through 5, you can simultaneously be working on steps 6 through 9.)

3. Pour off and discard the simmering water. Once again, cover the cod with cold tap water, bring the liquid to a boil, and gently simmer it for 10 minutes.

4. Transfer the cod pieces with a slotted spoon to several layers of paper towels and pat dry. Discard the water.

5. Skin and bone the cod. Reserve the fish for step 10.

6. Heat 3 tablespoons of the olive oil in a 2- to 3-quart saucepan over low to moderate heat.

7. Sauté the onions for 2 minutes. Add the garlic and sauté for 1 minute.

8. Add the wine promptly after completing step 7. Then add the tomatoes, Italian pepper, lemon juice, mint, and cayenne pepper. Mix the ingredients.

9. Bring the mixture to a simmer. Cook the sauce, uncovered, for 30 minutes over low heat.

10. Grease (with a dab of olive oil) the interior of a wide-bottomed 1½- to 2-quart casserole that can be used as the serving dish. Arrange the fish in the bottom of the pot. Pour the sauce over the cod.

11. Bring the preparation to a simmer. Cover, and cook the dish for 30 minutes over low heat.

12. Arrange the lemon slices on top of the *bacalao a la vizcaína* and sprinkle it with the parsley. Serve immediately.

Additional Keys to Success

If your kitchen is exceptionally warm and you don't have a cool spot in your home, place the soaking salt cod in the warmest part of your refrigerator. ❡ Should the fish float to the surface of the water during step 1, weight it down with a noncorrosible weight such as heavy porcelain plates. ❡ To help prevent the fish from sticking during step 11, periodically jerk the pan vigorously back and forth.

Serving Suggestions and Affinities

Serve plain boiled rice and/or crusty bread. ❡ Both beer and an everyday, assertive, dry white jug wine marry well with *bacalao a la vizcaína.*

Variations on a Theme

Don't skin the salt cod. ¶ Substitute sliced red bell pepper for all or a portion of the tomatoes.

Mail-Order Source

Salt cod is available through the mail from Casa Moneo Spanish Imports, 210 West 14th Street, New York, New York 10011 (212-929-1644).

◆§ Bobotie   *Serves 4 to 6*
(boh-ʙoo-tee)

The fairest part of South Africa is the sixty-mile-long Cape area, from Table Top Mountain to the Cape of Good Hope, where the cool Atlantic and warm Indian oceans embrace. I drove through this gorgeous landscape in October (springtime in the Southern Hemisphere) when hundreds of rare species of flowering plants were in bloom on hilly slopes and along the breathtaking cliff-edged coastline. Here and there were homes built in the Cape Dutch style, embellished with scrolled gables and made cheerful with white limewashed walls.

During this journey I met a Cape Malay whose ancestors came as slaves to these shores, centuries ago, from Malaya. The names of his forebears have long been forgotten, but not their culinary philosophy. Many a dish in South Africa is flavored with bold and aromatic seasonings typical of the Malayan cuisine. One of these South African specialties is *bobotie.*

"*Bobotie* resembles the *moussaka* of Greece," my Cape Malay friend said. "But we think ours is more interesting — it's the curry and dried fruits we put in it that make the difference." His wife's *bobotie* made the point even clearer.

2 slices white bread
1¼ cups milk
2½ tablespoons unsalted butter
1 cup chopped white onions
1 peeled and diced medium-sized baking apple
3 tablespoons fresh lemon juice
1 tablespoon grated lemon rind
3 tablespoons chopped dried apricots

3 tablespoons seedless raisins
3 tablespoons chopped blanched almonds
2 tablespoons curry powder
½ teaspoon salt (or to taste)
¼ teaspoon freshly ground black pepper
1½ pounds ground lean lamb
2 bay leaves
Yolks of 2 large eggs

Steps

1. Preheat the oven to 325° F.

2. Trim and quarter the bread slices. Soak the pieces in the milk for a quick second on each side. After gently squeezing out the excess milk, tear the pieces into small bits and set them aside. Reserve the milk for step 9.

3. Melt 2 tablespoons of the butter in a thick, wide-bottomed sauté pan over low heat.

4. Sauté the onions for 2 minutes. Add the apple and sauté the mixture for 1 minute.

5. Stir in the bread, lemon juice, lemon rind, apricots, raisins, almonds, curry powder, salt, and pepper. Add the lamb and cook the mixture for 3 minutes, stirring constantly.

6. Grease a 1½- to 2-quart soufflé or other baking dish with the remaining butter.

7. Transfer the meat mixture to the dish and bury the bay leaves in it. To help prevent the meat from forming a dome as it cooks, press down the mixture to form a slightly concave surface (the depression should be about ¼ inch deep).

8. Bake the dish in the middle of the oven for 20 to 25 minutes, depending on the depth of the meat mixture.

9. Beat the egg yolks and blend them into the reserved milk. Slowly pour the milk mixture over the meat mixture.

10. Bake the dish for 25 minutes more, or until the custard (egg-milk mixture) sets. Serve immediately.

Additional Keys to Success

When grating the lemon rind, do not cut into the bitter-flavored whitish pith. ¶ Use a fresh, top-quality brand of curry powder. Even better, blend your own. ¶ The meat must be lean. Otherwise, an undesirable layer of fat will rise to the surface as the dish bakes.

Serving Suggestions and Affinities

Plain rice is the usual starch accompaniment. ¶ Serve chutney on the side. ¶ Serve the dish with beer or a hearty red wine.

Variations on a Theme

Substitute beef, kid, or game meat for the lamb. Some cooks make *bobotie* with a combination of shrimp and firm-fleshed fish. ¶ Sauté the meat in hot oil or butter before baking it. Reduce the baking time. ¶ Substitute lemon or orange leaves for the bay leaves. Lemon grass is another alternative. ¶ Use 1 tablespoon of *atjar* (a pickled relish) rather than the lemon rind in step 5.

Mail-Order Sources

Curry powder, chutney, and *atjar* are available through the mail from Kalustyan Orient Expert Trading Corporation, 123 Lexington Avenue, New York, New York 10016 (212-685-3416). Lemon grass is available from Lynwood Market, 11325 Atlantic Avenue, Lynwood, California 90262 (213-635-9457).

◥ Bubble and Squeak   *Serves 2*

Some 50 miles northwest of London lies Oxford, the home of an internationally acclaimed seat of learning. Through seven centuries, Oxford University has nurtured the minds of celebrated English men and women too numerous to count. This roster of the great continues to grow; recent prime ministers Anthony Eden, Edward Heath, Harold Macmillan, Harold Wilson, and Margaret Thatcher all sharpened their wits in one or another of the university's twenty-three colleges.

I was well aware of Oxford's role in shaping English history when I explored the libraries and quadrangles of the various colleges and hopped from pub to pub to meet the latest generation of Oxford scholars. One of the lads I befriended invited me to his cousin's farmhouse in the rural Cherwell Valley, north of the town.

The day was Monday and, therefore, appropriate for his country cousin to be cooking bubble and squeak, a mixture of leftover roast beef and potatoes from the Sunday family meal I had missed. As the dish fries in the skillet, it bubbles and squeaks; hence its whimsical name.

Bubble and squeak is to me one of many fine examples of how a leftover dish can be greater than the sum of its parts. While bubble and squeak is certainly not a preparation to serve for a special occasion, it is as tasty a casual dish as you are likely to encounter anywhere.

2½ cups shredded cabbage
½ pound leftover cooked beef
3 tablespoons unsalted butter
¼ cup sliced white onions
½ cup leftover mashed potatoes
⅛ teaspoon freshly ground black pepper
Salt to taste (see below)

Steps

1. Add the cabbage to a pot of boiling water and simmer for 5 minutes. Drain and squeeze reasonably dry.
2. Slice the meat into thin strips.
3. Melt the butter in a skillet. Add the onions and sauté them over low to moderate heat for about 2 minutes, stirring constantly.
4. Mix the cabbage and then the potatoes into the onions. Cook this mixture for about 3 minutes, stirring occasionally.
5. Combine into the mixture the meat, pepper, and salt (the quantity of salt will depend on the saltiness of your leftover meat). Cook for about 2 minutes, turning the preparation every 30 seconds.
6. Serve mounded in a warm bowl.

Additional Keys to Success

Leftover corned beef is particularly suited for this dish. Very little salt will be needed if you use corned beef. ¶ The cabbage will become malodorous if overcooked.

Variations on a Theme

Substitute leftover Brussels sprouts for the cabbage. ¶ Some cooks prepare bubble and squeak without the meat or without the potatoes, using one or the other. ¶ For a coarser-textured bubble and squeak, use leftover whole potatoes that have been slightly mashed. ¶ Prepare bubble and squeak pancake-style by frying it on each side until crisp and brown.

✌§ Bul-gogi   *Serves 4*
(buhl-go-kee)

My senses will never forget that sunny winter afternoon outside an old stone farmhouse within a day's jaunt of Seoul, South Korea. Though I stood shivering on a weathered granite doorstep, my gastronomic heart was enkindled by a captivating sight. A few feet from me, a wizened peasant woman was barbecuing thin strips of marinated beef on an iron grill that was solidly secured, home-style, on top of a pit of hot ash-dusted coals that sent reassuring wisps of cottony steam skyward into the crisp air. She was doing her best to teach me her version of the tasty and aromatic *bul-gogi* ("fire beef"). She was one of those strong-willed countrypersons who speak with a commanding voice softened by gentle eyes. In this way, she instructed me.

The old woman's cooking did nothing to disprove my belief that Koreans are the barbecuing masters of the world. The Koreans' favorite ingredient for the searing grate is beef; unlike most Asians, Koreans prefer that meat to pork. *Bul-gogi* not only features the flesh of the bovine, it also embraces two other Korean mainstays, garlic and sesame seeds. Typical it is.

1½ pounds beef top round
¼ cup soy sauce
3 tablespoons rice vinegar
3 tablespoons sesame oil
2 tablespoons toasted sesame
  seeds
1 teaspoon sugar

3 tablespoons finely minced
  scallions
1½ tablespoons finely minced
  garlic
½ teaspoon freshly ground black
  pepper

Steps

1. Cut the beef on the diagonal into flat ⅛-inch-thick slices, about 3 to 5 inches long by 1½ inches wide. Place the pieces in a noncorrosible bowl.

2. Add the remaining ingredients, one by one, to the bowl. Using your fingers, mix the preparation gently but thoroughly.

3. Cover the bowl and place it in the refrigerator for 12 to 24 hours. Mix the preparation occasionally.

4. Remove the bowl from the refrigerator at least 1 hour before cooking the marinated beef.

5. Drain the beef before cooking, being careful not to press out its succulent juices or to rub off the clinging sesame seeds. Discard the marinade, or reserve it for future sauce making.

6. Barbecue the marinated beef slices in a single layer (the slices should not touch each other) over hot coals for 25 to 40 seconds per side, depending on the thickness of the meat and intensity of the heat.

7. Serve the *bul-gogi* immediately.

Additional Keys to Success

Buy top round that is 1 to 1¼ inches thick. ¶ Trim the meat of all fat and connective tissue. ¶ If rice vinegar is unavailable, substitute cider vinegar or white wine vinegar. ¶ The longer you marinate the beef slices, the more tender and flavorful they will become. ¶ Unless the meat is brought to room temperature in step 4, the exterior of the slices will probably be overcooked by the time the interior is done. ¶ If your sesame seeds are untoasted, bake them in a single layer in a pan in a preheated 350° F oven for approximately 15 minutes; then let them cool. ¶ Once the *bul-gogi* is cooked, it must not be allowed to cool. If you are cooking more than one batch, keep the cooked portions warm.

Serving Suggestions and Affinities

Classic accompaniments include white rice, green vegetables, and — if you have it — Korea's fiery pickled vegetable preparation called *kim chee*. ¶ Drink beer with *bul-gogi*. Or, if you prefer, try a robust red wine such as a California Zinfandel. ¶ Serve fresh fruit for dessert.

Variations on a Theme

You can substitute flank, sirloin, or filet steak for the top round. The flank will be more flavorful but less tender; the sirloin and filet will be more tender but less flavorful. ¶ Some cooks prepare *bul-gogi* using ground or crushed sesame seeds, but whole seeds will give your finished dish more visual and tactile character. ¶ If you don't have a barbecue, cook the meat on a grate in a pan under a preheated oven broiler.

Mail-Order Source

Rice vinegar, sesame oil, sesame seeds, and *kim chee* are available through the mail from Katagiri & Company, 224 East 59th Street, New York, New York 10022 (212-755-3566).

◄§ Carbonnade Flamande   *Serves 4 to 6*
(kahr-buhn-NAHD flah-MAHND)

Belgium is really two countries in one. To the south (the inland half of the nation) live the French-speaking Walloons, who favor wine and Gallic-style cuisine. The culinary preferences of the Flemish-speaking people — who live in the northern, or North Sea coastal, half of Belgium — are different. Like their Dutch neighbors, the Flemish of Belgium relish a heartier fare and quaff beers of many brewing styles.

Beer is also used in the kitchen in Flanders. Cooks pour it into many preparations, including *carbonnade flamande,* one of the world's tastiest beer-infused dishes.

I learned this recipe for the beer-and-onion-rich *carbonnade flamande* on a small farm within sight of the famous thirteenth-century belfry of Bruges, the picturesque medieval merchant city that once wielded substantial wealth and trading muscle around the globe. Today, Bruges has many reminders of its glorious past, including a number of well-preserved public buildings and peaked red-roofed houses in the medieval mode. There's even a tree-lined canal or two, remnants of the fourteenth-century days when a complicated maze of waterways connected this "Venice of the North" to the seven seas.

12 ounces dark beer
1 cup unseasoned beef stock (see page 195)
⅓ cup diced salt pork
2 pounds cubed lean beef chuck or round
3 cups sliced yellow onions
1 teaspoon minced garlic
1½ tablespoons vinegar
1 tablespoon chopped fresh parsley
1 teaspoon summer savory
1 bay leaf
¼ teaspoon cinnamon
¼ teaspoon freshly ground black pepper
6 slices whole-wheat bread
Prepared mustard

Steps

1. Bring the beer and stock to room temperature.
2. Preheat the oven to 300° F.
3. Render the salt pork in a 4- to 5-quart casserole over moderate heat. With a slotted spoon, transfer the solid pieces to a warm plate.
4. Brown the beef in the hot fat on all sides (allow 2 to 3 minutes per batch). As you brown each batch, transfer it to the plate containing the salt pork.
5. Reduce the heat to low to moderate. Add the onions and sauté them for about 4 minutes, stirring frequently.
6. Add the garlic and sauté the mixture for 1 minute, stirring constantly. Immediately pour in the beer. Add the stock and vinegar. Stir the preparation and bring it to a simmer.
7. Return the meat to the pot. Stir the ingredients.
8. Cover the casserole and place it in the middle of the oven. Bake for 1½ hours.
9. Stir into the preparation the parsley, savory, bay leaf, cinnamon, and black pepper.
10. Trim the bread of its crust. Spread a thin layer of mustard on both slices of the bread, and lay it on top of the preparation. Stir it as you submerge and partially break up the bread. Cover, and continue to bake the dish for 30 additional minutes.
11. Lightly stir the *carbonnade flamande,* discard the bay leaf, and serve immediately.

Additional Keys to Success

If you don't add the beer immediately in step 5, the garlic may burn and therefore become bitter. ¶ For flavor's sake, use a top-quality brand of beer.

Serving Suggestions and Affinities

Boiled peeled potatoes are the traditional accompaniment. Also serve a side dish of steamed and buttered baby carrots. ¶ Beer, of course, is the customary beverage.

Variations on a Theme

Carbonnade flamande is a perfect dish to use flat, leftover beer, as long as that beverage has been stored in the refrigerator. ¶ If a milder-flavored *carbonnade flamande* is desired, use a pilsner-type lager instead of the dark beer. ¶ Substitute thyme for the savory. ¶ In step 9, cut the bread into 1½-inch squares and neatly arrange them on top of the stew. Slightly moisten the bread with the sauce. Bake uncovered (so that the bread will partially toast) for 30 minutes.

Leftovers

Cook *carbonnade flamande* with leftovers in mind. A day or two in the refrigerator will add new flavor dimensions.

Mail-Order Source

Summer savory is available through the mail from H. Roth & Son, 1577 First Avenue, New York, New York, 10028 (212-734-1110).

⋅§ Cassoulet   *Serves 8*
(kahs-soo-LAY)

Languedoc, the home of *cassoulet*! In southwestern France the independent-minded peasants created a bean dish worthy of the highest epicurean honors.

Several years ago I realized a suppressed desire: I drove through the back roads of rural Languedoc in search of the perfect *cassoulet*.

My itinerary also took me through the crowded streets of Toulouse, Castelnaudary, and Carcassonne because these three cities are touted as having the finest urban *cassoulets* in Languedoc. My taste buds discovered an even better source of the citified *cassoulet*: Villefranche de Lauragais. It lies in the *cassoulet* corridor between Toulouse and Castelnaudary. Please keep it a secret.

Farmhouse *cassoulets* are even more exciting, perhaps because these renditions are less codified. Each cook has his own cast of ingredients — in some pots smoked pork is the star, but in others it may be goose, duck, lamb, mutton, sausages, or another meat.

Many armchair gourmets insist that if the dish is to be accorded the appellation *cassoulet*, it must contain *confit d'oie* (preserved goose). Not so. Though the vast majority of *cassoulets* in Languedoc contained this ingredient, I came across several equally authentic and ambrosial versions prepared without it. This is fortunate for American cooks, because *confit d'oie* is hard to come by in this country. When it is available, *confit d'oie* is usually canned and, as such, is apt to degrade more than improve your dish. It's also ridiculously expensive.

What's essential to a good *cassoulet* is slow cooking. Should the liquid boil, the beans will burst and begin to lose their skins.

2 pounds dried white beans
1 4-pound duckling
1 pound fresh pork shoulder
1 cup chopped white onions
2 tablespoons minced garlic
1 cup chopped tomatoes
1 cup dry white wine
3 tablespoons fresh lemon juice
2 bay leaves
1 heaping teaspoon thyme
1 heaping teaspoon ground sage
¼ teaspoon ground cloves
¼ cup chopped fresh parsley

½ teaspoon freshly ground black pepper
2 cups unseasoned chicken stock (see page 195)
1 pound garlicky, firm pork sausage
1 pound well-smoked boneless ham
½ pound fatback
2 tablespoons unsalted butter
1 cup unseasoned coarse bread crumbs
Salt to taste (see step 12)

Steps

1. Spread the beans, one layer at a time, on a large, flat platter. Look for and remove any foreign substances, such as stones.

2. Place the beans in a large stainless steel, glass, or enamel bowl. Add enough cold tap water to cover them by 2 to 3 inches. Soak overnight, changing the water at least once.

3. Cut up the duckling into eight pieces and the pork into 1½-inch cubes. Cut up the excess fat of the duckling and pork and render it in a 7- to 8-quart casserole over moderate heat. In several batches, sauté the duckling and pork for about 5 minutes, or until each piece is lightly brown. Transfer the pieces to a warm platter.

4. Add the onions to the pan and reduce the heat to low to moderate. Sauté the onions for 2 minutes, stirring frequently.

5. Add the garlic and sauté for 1 minute.

6. Add the tomatoes, wine, lemon juice, bay leaves, thyme, sage, cloves, parsley, and pepper. Stir well. Gently simmer the mixture, uncovered, for 30 minutes, stirring occasionally.

7. Preheat the oven to 300° F.

8. Discard the bay leaves. Drain the beans and add them to the pot. Also add the duckling and pork from the platter, as well as the chicken stock.

9. Slice the sausage into ¼-inch-thick rounds. Cut the ham into ½-inch cubes and the fatback into ¼-inch cubes. Stir these ingredients into the casserole.

10. Cover the casserole and bake it in the middle of the oven for 2½ hours. Stir the preparation every hour.

11. Melt the butter in a medium-sized skillet over low to moderate heat. When the foam of the butter begins to subside, add the bread crumbs. Sauté them for 3 minutes, or until they become lightly brown.

12. Remove the casserole from the oven. Stir the ingredients. Taste for salt. Stir in the needed salt (the quantity you add will mainly depend upon the inherent saltiness of the sausage and ham — you'll probably need about ½ teaspoon). Layer the bread crumbs over the top. Return the casserole to the oven, raise the temperature to 325° F and bake, uncovered, for 30 minutes.

13. Remove the casserole from the oven. Push the crust down into the bean and meat mixture. Serve promptly.

Additional Keys to Success

The traditional bean — the white haricot bean of France — is not easily obtained in America. The best substitute is the Great Northern bean. ¶ The soaking beans will double in volume, so be sure to use a large enough bowl and sufficient water. ¶ By changing the water in step 2, you minimize the flatulent effect of the beans. ¶ If you can make your own *confit d'oie* or *confit de canard,* by all means substitute it for the duckling in this recipe. ¶ To help prevent the garlic from burning and thereby becoming bitter, proceed promptly from step 5 to step 6. ¶ If fresh vine-ripened tomatoes are unavailable, substitute canned imported Italian plum tomatoes. ¶ The traditional casserole for the *cassoulet* is earthenware. ¶ Select a garlicky sausage, such as kielbasa. ¶ Should you add the salt at the beginning of the recipe, the bean skins will unnecessarily toughen.

Serving Suggestions and Affinities

A *cassoulet* can be a meal all by itself, but a green salad on the side does the "pride of Languedoc" justice. ¶ Serve a medium-bodied red wine with some acidity — Languedoc, the wine of the region, complements its gastronomic compatriot admirably.

Variations on a Theme

Experiment with other meats. How about fresh lamb or mutton, fresh or smoked goose or game birds, calves' feet, veal or pork breast, pork rind, smoked pig's cheek, or ham hocks? ¶ After pushing the crust into the bean and meat mixture, return the casserole to the oven and let a new crust form. Repeat this cycle two or three times.

Leftovers

A *cassoulet* is a natural leftover dish, as its flavor improves each time it is stored and reheated. Therefore, make more than you plan to eat the first day. ¶ As the quantity of the *cassoulet* dwindles, transfer it to a smaller casserole.

Mail-Order Source

Sage is available through the mail from H. Roth & Son, 1577 First Avenue, New York, New York 10028 (212-734-1110).

⌐§ Cha Chiang Mien   *Serves 4*
(chah chung min)

This recipe for *cha chiang mien*, egg noodles with stir-fried pork, is one of the culinary treasures I brought back with me from China. I happened upon it through one of those chains of events that often lead a traveler from one pleasant experience to another.

During my stay in Hangzhou, I took a side trip to the gently rolling hills in the countryside to visit the Lung Ching (Dragon Well) tea plantation. The journey was something of a pilgrimage for me, because Dragon Well has long been my favorite green tea.

A worker-guide gave me a morning's tour of the plantation, showing me how the tea is grown, harvested, and processed. When she discovered how much I appreciated Dragon Well tea, she covertly slipped me a small packet of the commune's very best tea, the number-one tea out of sixteen possible grades. She advised me to take a half-hour's ride to Running Tiger Spring. There, she explained, I could ask the attendant at the teahouse to brew this choice Dragon Well tea in water that has such high density and surface tension it seems to defy gravity. As I later saw with my own eyes, you can pour the famous Running Tiger Spring water into a glass to a level of about one third of an inch above the rim before it starts to overflow.

Next to my table at the teahouse sat an English-speaking resident of Hangzhou with whom I shared my once-in-a-lifetime pot of tea. We struck up a conversation and quickly discovered that we were both interested in Chinese gastronomy. When I told him of my interest in peasant cooking, he invited me to his house to try *cha chiang mien*, prepared by his cook, who came from a peasant family. "Yes," I responded without hesitation, and that evening I was in possession of the recipe for this informal yet tempting dish.

⅔ pound ground lean pork
2 tablespoons sesame oil
⅔ pound Oriental dried egg
  noodles
2 tablespoons peanut (or other
  vegetable) oil

1 teaspoon coarsely minced
  garlic
3 tablespoons thickly sliced
  scallions
1 tablespoon coarsely minced
  fresh ginger

1 tablespoon minced fermented
  black beans
4 teaspoons soy sauce

2 tablespoons rice (or wine)
  vinegar
¼ cup unseasoned chicken stock
  (see page 195)

Steps

1. Bring the pork to room temperature. Bring 4 quarts of water and the sesame oil to a rolling boil in a 6-quart pot over high heat.

2. Add the egg noodles to the boiling water and cook them for 3 minutes, or according to package directions. Drain the noodles and transfer them to a warm bowl of sufficient size to accommodate the tossing task in step 7. Cover the bowl and reserve for step 7.

3. Heat the peanut oil in a wok over moderate heat.

4. Add the pork and stir-fry the preparation for 3 minutes, breaking up the lumps as you cook the meat.

5. Add the garlic, scallions, ginger, and black beans, and stir-fry the ingredients for 1 minute.

6. Pour the soy sauce, vinegar, and chicken stock into the meat mixture. Cook it for 3 minutes, stirring frequently.

7. Spoon the pork sauce over the noodles. Toss the ingredients before transferring them to individual bowls or plates, and serve immediately.

Additional Keys to Success

If you don't have sesame oil, substitute vegetable oil. Some type of oil is essential, because it helps keep the noodles from sticking together as they cook and as they sit in the serving bowl. ¶ Do not overcook the noodles in step 2 or they will become mushy. ¶ When stir-frying in steps 4 and 5, constantly toss the ingredients in the oil in the bottom of the wok. ¶ Black bean sauce may be substituted for the black beans if it is not overly seasoned.

Serving Suggestions and Affinities

Cha chiang mien is an ideal one-dish quick lunch for a nonsummer day. ¶ Accompany the noodles with a hot clear soup. ¶ Conclude the meal with fresh fruit followed by tea.

Variations on a Theme

Add to your preparation one or more of the following vegetables, cut in julienne strips: bamboo shoots, carrots, cucumbers, or white radishes. Bean sprouts are another possibility. ¶ Substitute chili oil for the sesame oil.

Mail-Order Source

Oriental dried egg noodles, sesame oil, fresh ginger, fermented black beans, rice vinegar, black bean sauce, and chili oil are available through the mail from Katagiri & Company, 224 East 59th Street, New York, New York 10022 (212-755-3566).

⤝ Ching Yu   *Serves 2*
(JING yooh)

Of all the cuisines of China, Cantonese is the most delicate. The aim of the cook is to enhance the natural flavor of the main ingredients. To achieve that goal, the cook starts off with ingredients in top condition — and keeps the quantity and type of flavoring agents in check lest they mask the flavor of the principal components of the dish.

This recipe for *ching yu* (steamed fish) illustrates the Cantonese talent for subtle cooking. I learned it in a small farming village outside Canton.

The peasant cook who taught me how to prepare the dish lived with her family in a small, mud-walled and tile-roofed dwelling that opened onto a courtyard shared by several other families. Inside her home, the floor was pounded earth and the furnishings were sparse — a table, four chairs, two mattresses, and the traditional wood-burning oven upon which she placed her wok and bamboo steamer for cooking a fish.

She fetched her fish — fresh and flipping — from a pond beyond a copse of trees. "Our commune is self-sufficient," she said proudly. "Rice, vegetables, chickens, pigs, and fish — we have them all." She also had reason to be proud of her recipe for steamed fish.

1½-pound dressed whole fish	½ teaspoon soy sauce
2 tablespoons slivered scallions	½ teaspoon rice vinegar
2 tablespoons slivered fresh ginger	1 teaspoon minced fermented black beans

Steps

1. Remove the fish from the refrigerator approximately 45 minutes before starting step 2.
2. Bring to a boil 1 to 2 inches of water in a large steamer (or a wok or other suitably sized pot) that has a flat steaming rack.
3. Grease the steaming rack if it is not made of wood.
4. Place a third of the scallions and ginger on the steaming rack where the fish will lie.
5. Make three shallow diagonal slashes approximately 1 inch apart on both sides of the fish. These slashes, which should be about 2 to 3 inches in length, should extend from about ½ inch above the opening of the belly cavity to ½ inch below the top of the fish.
6. Mix the soy sauce, rice vinegar, and fermented black beans in a small bowl. Using your fingers, thoroughly rub the fish's exterior and cavity with the mixture.
7. Stuff the cavity of the fish with a third of the scallions and ginger. Place the fish on the previously arranged bed of scallions and ginger.
8. Arrange the remaining slivers of scallions and ginger on top of the fish in a neat crisscross pattern.
9. Place the fish and its steaming rack in the pot. Cover the pot. Steam the fish over moderate to high heat for 8 to 10 minutes per inch of maximum thickness (a 1½-inch-thick fish, for example, will take 12 to 15 minutes) or until the flesh of the thickest part of the fish flakes when pried apart with a pair of chopsticks or forks.
10. Transfer the fish to a warm plate (or simply place the steaming rack on top of a warm plate). Serve immediately.

Additional Keys to Success

Suitable fish that come in 1½-pound dressed whole weights include red snapper, sea bass, and sea bream. ❡ A fish cooked with its head and tail intact is more flavorful, so think twice before removing those parts of the anatomy. ❡ Substitute a lightly seasoned black bean sauce or an extra ½ teaspoon of soy sauce if fermented black beans are unavailable. ❡ If you don't own a suitable steamer (or a wok with a lid and perforated tray), improvise one. You'll need a shallow, wide-bottomed pot that has a tight-fitting lid and a large, rimmed, flat, heat-proof plate that should be at least 1 inch smaller than the pot. (The space is needed so that the steam can better envelop the fish.) Bring to a boil at least 1 inch of water in the pot. In the middle of the water place a trivet or similar platform that is sufficiently large to support the plate stably and to keep the plate at least 1 inch above the water line. Lightly oil the top surface of the plate and cautiously place it on the trivet. Carefully place the fish on top of the plate and cover the pot. Steam the fish for about 12 minutes per inch of thickness (you'll need the extra time because less steam reaches the fish when you use a plate than when you use a conventional perforated steaming rack). ¶ The slashes serve a practical purpose. They better enable the taste and fragrance of the flavoring agents to penetrate the flesh of the fish — but if the slashes are too deep, too much of the fish's juices will be lost during the steaming process. ¶ In step 8, arrange the slivers in the middle of the fish so that they won't fall off when you remove the fish and rack from the pot. ¶ Keep the lid on the pot during the entire steaming period. Otherwise, much of the steam will escape.

Serving Suggestions and Affinities

Rice is the traditional accompaniment. ¶ Serve a green vegetable such as snow peas or broccoli. ¶ In China, a light soup is the most popular beverage accompaniment. Tea is imbibed before or after, but seldom during, a meal.

Variations on a Theme

Stuff the cavity with reconstituted dried mushrooms. ¶ Prepare a dipping sauce for the fish. ¶ Substitute Shaohsing wine for the vinegar.

Mail-Order Source

Fresh ginger, rice vinegar, fermented black beans, black bean sauce, and dried mushrooms are available through the mail from Katagiri & Company, 224 East 59th Street, New York, New York 10022 (212-755-3566).

◄§ Choucroute Garnie   *Serves 6*
(shoo-KROOT gahr-NEE)

Alsace is the postcard province of France. Between the German border on the Rhine and the pine-clad Vosges Mountains lies a necklace of medieval villages sporting cobblestone streets lined with half-timbered houses. Potted plants in full bloom adorn the overhanging balconies. If I were ever asked to make a film of *Cinderella,* I would shoot it in Riquewihr, the fairest village of them all.

Riquewihr and its sister villages are surrounded chiefly by vineyards. Occasionally you see a farm populated with disgruntled pigs and squawking geese who almost seem to know their culinary destinies.

Most of the citizens are bilingual; they speak French and German, sometimes switching from one language to another in midsentence. The German heritage in Alsace can also be detected at the dinner table. Wines made from Riesling and Sylvaner grapes are popular and come in tall, slender, green-tinted bottles similar to those from the Mosel wine district. *Choucroute garnie* and many other local specialties are robust and hearty.

I rented the top floor of a house in Riquewihr with windows revealing rolling hills covered with vines. Since the owner of the land and building vinted and bottled his product in the basement, I had no worries about a wine "not traveling well" here. I had only to walk down two flights of stairs to buy a bottle of Gewürztraminer, the spicy wine that is the oenological trademark of Alsace.

My temporary abode had a spotless kitchen equipped with a gas stove and oversized pot perfectly proportioned for the *choucroute garnie* that I had in mind. All I lacked was a local culinary mentor and the ingredients.

By making inquiries around the village, I was able to find a seasoned cook who was willing to share with me some of the insights she learned from preparing *choucroute garnie* at least once a month for a decade. She itemized the ingredients, and with her shopping list in hand, I drove thirty miles to the charming town of Colmar, noted for its food market. Strolling from shop to shop, I gradually filled my arms with the finest of foods for the *choucroute garnie.* I dashed back to Riquewihr to pick up my teacher. The two of us spent the rest of the afternoon making a marvelous *choucroute garnie.* As we waited for the dish to cook to perfection, we sipped several glasses of Gewürztraminer while listening to Bach's Brandenburg Concerti.

4 slices bacon
6 medium-sized mushrooms
1 medium-sized carrot
1 medium-sized baking apple
1½ cups sliced white onions
1½ cups dry white wine
1½ cups water
2 bay leaves
1 teaspoon thyme
2 tablespoons chopped fresh
    parsley

12 juniper berries (or 2
    tablespoons caraway seeds)
Heaping ½ teaspoon salt (or to
    taste)
¼ teaspoon freshly ground black
    pepper
2 pounds sauerkraut
Smoked pork (see Additional
    Keys to Success)
12 small boiling potatoes

Steps

1. Preheat the oven to 300° F.
2. Dice the bacon and partially render it for several minutes in a 4- to 5-quart casserole over low to moderate heat.
3. Chop the mushrooms. Peel and dice the carrot. Peel, core, and dice the apple.
4. Sauté the onions in the casserole for 3 minutes over low heat, stirring frequently. Add the mushroom, carrot, and apple pieces. Sauté the mixture for 5 minutes, stirring frequently.
5. Stir in the wine, water, bay leaves, thyme, parsley, juniper berries, salt, and pepper. Bring the mixture to a simmer.
6. Drain, rinse, and drain the sauerkraut. Stir it into the casserole. Mix in the smoked pork ingredients, making certain that all are covered by the sauerkraut.
7. Bake the preparation, covered, in the middle of the oven for 2 hours. Stir the ingredients midway through the cooking process.
8. Peel the potatoes. Submerge them in the sauerkraut and continue baking the dish for 30 to 40 additional minutes, depending on the diameter of the potatoes.
9. Transfer the sauerkraut with a slotted spoon to the middle of a

large, nonflat serving platter. Shape it into a neat pile. Arrange the pork and potatoes around this mound. Serve immediately.

Additional Keys to Success

You need not rinse the sauerkraut if it is freshly made. (Fresh sauerkraut can sometimes be found in this country in Jewish or Middle-European markets. ¶ Alsatian peasant cooks vary their selection of smoked pork according to availability. Typically, they add two or more of these varieties of smoked pork: sausages, shoulder, bacon, ham hocks, chops, and loin. They sometimes also add pickled pig's feet, fresh pork, or smoked game animals and birds. Create your own formulation for this recipe, using a total of about 2 pounds boneless meat or 3 to 4 pounds bone-in meat.

Serving Suggestions and Affinities

Steamed or simmered kale is a traditional side dish. Pumpernickel, rye, or crusty French bread almost always accompanies *choucroute garnie*. ¶ Because this dish is high in acidity, few wines, save the spicy Alsatian Gewürztraminer, are assertive enough to stand up to a *choucroute garnie*. Beer is by far the most popular beverage choice. ¶ Follow the meal with a glass of kirschwasser or other eau de vie.

Leftovers

Choucroute garnie develops new and intriguing flavors when it is refrigerated and reheated. Make plenty. ¶ Add leftover meats such as roast lamb or braised veal to the pot of leftover *choucroute garnie*.

Mail-Order Source

Juniper berries and caraway seeds are available through the mail from H. Roth & Son, 1577 First Avenue, New York, New York 10028 (212-734-1110).

⋖§ Cotriade
(koh-tree-AHD)

Serves 4

The passport of a denizen of Brittany says the owner is French; the hearts of most of these sturdy folk will tell you they are Bretons, an independent-minded people descended from the Celts, who first emerged in this region before the time of Julius Caesar.

Celtic customs have not succumbed to the ages. I've visited villages where the preferred language is not French but Breton, which is related to the traditional tongues of Ireland, Wales, and Scotland. Still standing in open fields are megaliths erected by the ancient Druids and grass-roofed burial mounds of long-forgotten Celtic nobles.

The massive Brittany peninsula juts into the sea, framing the northern boundary of the Bay of Biscay and the southern limits of the English Channel. The steep coastline is penetrated by awesome inlets where thunderous waves hurl themselves against unyielding jagged rocks, creating a rhythmical sound soothing and reassuring to the soul. Beyond the promontory in the churning sea, I spotted small fishing boats manned by oilskin-clad sailors returning to their ports with an assortment of fish. Part of this catch, I'm sure, was transformed into *cotriade*, "the *bouillabaisse* of Bretagne."

As in Marseilles, the home of *bouillabaisse*, arguments abound in Brittany as to which fish should and shouldn't go into an authentic *cotriade*. Most Breton cooks take the "more the merrier" approach, as long as lobster and other shellfish don't enter the pot. Other local cooks freely add mussels and other mollusks to their multifish *cotriade*, while still others concoct single-fish versions.

Over the course of several trips to Brittany, I've eaten *cotriades* made with all manner of fish, including bass, cod, eel, hake, halibut, John Dory, mackerel, red mullet, sardines, swordfish, and a few whose identities to this day remain a mystery to me. Generally, I prefer those *cotriades* prepared with lean fish (cod, for example) because oily fish (such as sardines) taste much better when cooked with dry rather than moist heat.

2 tablespoons unsalted butter
½ cup chopped white onions
4 cups unseasoned fish stock (see page 196)
¾ cup dry white wine
6 peeled and quartered medium-sized boiling potatoes
2 tablespoons white vinegar
1 bay leaf
½ teaspoon dried thyme
¼ teaspoon dried summer savory
⅛ teaspoon freshly grated nutmeg
½ teaspoon salt (or to taste)
¼ teaspoon freshly ground black pepper
2½ pounds assorted fish (see recipe introduction)
8 ¼-inch-thick French bread slices, crusts removed
1 teaspoon chopped fresh parsley

Steps

1. Melt the butter in a wide-bottomed 3- to 4-quart casserole. When the foam begins to subside, add the onions. Sauté them for 2 minutes, stirring frequently.

2. Stir in the stock and wine. Bring the liquid to a boil and add the potatoes, vinegar, bay leaf, thyme, savory, nutmeg, salt, and pepper. Bring the liquid to a simmer. Continue to simmer, covered, for 10 to 15 minutes, depending on the thickness of the potatoes.

3. Lay the fish on top of the potatoes. Cover and simmer for 5 to 12 minutes, depending on the thickness of the fish (if the thickness of the fish pieces varies markedly, give the thicker ones a head start).

4. Toast the bread. Line the bottom of a warm soup tureen with the toast.

5. Transfer the fish and potatoes to a warm serving platter. Sprinkle the potatoes with the parsley.

6. Strain the sauce into the tureen and bring it to the table. Serve the soup along with the fish and potatoes.

Additional Keys to Success

Cook with whole fish, fish fillets, or fish steaks — or a combination of them. If you use all boneless fish, buy only 1½ pounds. ¶ Do not let the liquid boil in step 2 (lest the fish stock develop an off-odor) or in step 3 (lest the fish break apart).

Serving Suggestions and Affinities

Arrange a low wall of half-slices of lemon between the fish and potatoes on the platter. ¶ Put a basket of crusty French bread on the table. ¶ A worthy beverage accompaniment for this fish stew is a Muscadet Sèvre-et-Maine or another similar dry white wine. Alternatively, serve hard cider.

Variations on a Theme

In step 2, substitute hard (not sweet) cider for the wine. ¶ Add diced carrots to the pot 5 minutes before you add the fish. Serve the carrots with the potatoes. ¶ Serve *cotriade* as two courses: soup (first) and fish and potatoes (second). Keep the latter warm in a preheated 200° F oven while you enjoy the soup. ¶ Serve *cotriade* as a one-dish meal in large soup bowls. In this case, cube the potatoes and simmer them for several minutes in step 2 — and cook only boned, bite-sized fish pieces in step 3.

Mail-Order Source

Summer savory is available through the mail from H. Roth & Son, 1577 First Avenue, New York, New York 10028 (212-734-1110).

⋚ Côte de Porc Normande   *Serves 4*
(koht duh POHR nohr-MAHND)

Normandy is at its scenic zenith in May. Most of the inland countryside is clothed with a blanket of new green grass punctuated by dairy cows. In the background a million apple trees have exploded with pink and white blossoms, infusing the air with their unmistakable fragrance.

Cows and apple trees, two of Normandy's symbols, are put to superb culinary use. From the cows come rich cream, an essential ingredient for many a Normandy sauce, for such cheeses as Camembert, and for some of the world's most laudable butter. From the fruit come hard cider and the finest apple brandy on earth, Calvados.

Côte de porc normande illustrates the sublime interplay between Calvados and the dairy products, cream and butter. Once you've fashioned a sauce with "Normandy lightning" you will probably want to keep a bottle of Calvados handy in your kitchen.

Calvados, of course, should not be reserved solely for culinary use. It has a traditional place on the Normandy table. A farmer introduced me to the custom of creating "the Norman hole" (*le trou normand*). Halfway through our meal, he invited me to join him in gulping a shot of Calvados. "It will make a hole in your stomach," he said, "for the remaining food." It's an amusing theory.

4 1½-inch-thick medium-sized pork chops
2 tablespoons unsalted butter
3 tablespoons chopped shallots
1 tablespoon Calvados
¼ teaspoon ground sage
⅛ teaspoon freshly grated nutmeg
¼ teaspoon salt (or to taste)
⅛ teaspoon freshly ground black pepper
¼ cup heavy cream

Steps

1. Remove the pork chops from the refrigerator 1 hour before starting step 2.
2. Melt the butter in a large, heavy-bottomed sauté pan over low to moderate heat. As soon as the foam of the butter starts to subside, add the pork chops and brown them for 2 minutes on each side.
3. Transfer the pork chops to a warm platter.
4. Add the shallots to the pan and sauté them for 1 minute. Stir frequently.
5. Remove the pan from the heat, wait 30 seconds, and then quickly stir in the Calvados, sage, nutmeg, salt, and pepper. Thoroughly stir in the cream and return the pan to the heat.
6. Return the chops to the pan and coat them on all sides with the sauce.
7. Cover the pan and braise the chops over low heat for 25 minutes, turning the chops halfway through the cooking process.
8. Transfer the chops to a warm serving platter or individual plates.
9. Turn up the heat to moderate. Cook the sauce for 1 minute, stirring constantly.
10. Pour the sauce over the chops. Serve immediately.

Additional Keys to Success

Don't substitute thinner pork chops — they won't cook to the same desirable degree of succulence. ¶ If you can't find Calvados, use high-quality applejack. ❡ The pork chops will toughen and the cream will curdle if the preparation boils even slightly during step 7. If your burner can't be adjusted to a low enough setting, use a heat diffuser. ❡ In step 7, keep the pot covered except when you are turning the chops. Otherwise, needed steam will escape.

Serving Suggestions and Affinities

Garnish the chops with parsley sprigs. ❡ Serve crusty white bread, a green salad, and steamed rice. ❡ Serve a dry, medium-bodied white wine such as Saint-Véran or California Chardonnay. Or sip Calvados.

Variations on a Theme

In step 4, after you sauté the shallots, temporarily remove them from the pan, and sauté some chopped or sliced mushrooms. ❡ Substitute 1½-inch-thick boneless pork loin slices for the chops. ❡ Rather than adding the Calvados, cream, nutmeg, and pepper in step 5, incorporate them in step 9. Begin step 9 by raising the heat to high. Add and ignite the Calvados. Reduce the heat to moderate. Add the cream, nutmeg, and pepper, stirring until the sauce thickens. Proceed to step 10.

❧ Couscous   *Serves 6 to 8*
(ᴋᴏᴏs-koos)

I ate my first *couscous* in an unbaked-brick farmhouse outside Tangiers on July 10, 1956. It was also the day Morocco regained its independence after nearly half a century under European domination.

Everywhere Moroccans were celebrating with unrestrained joy — and my host slaughtered one of his fatted lambs for the occasion. For the festive meal, he clad himself in his best *djellaba*, the traditional long-sleeved, hooded robe of his Berber ancestors. His wife was equally radiant in her hand-embroidered, head-to-toe *burkas.*

A lamb *couscous* was served. *Couscous,* the national dish of Morocco, consists of a mound of steamed pellets of semolina flour ringed with stewed meats and vegetables.

Moroccans generally prepare *couscous* in a special cooking vessel called a *couscousier.* It resembles an oversized, bulbous double boiler, except that the bottom of the upper pot (which holds the semolina pellets) is perforated. The holes allow the rising steam from the simmering stew in the lower pot to cook and flavor the pellets above.

Sometimes Moroccans make *couscous* without the *couscousier*. Since few Americans own this cooking utensil (and would not want to invest in one for infrequent use), I give the non-*couscousier* method in the accompanying recipe.

If you do have a genuine *couscousier*, use it, as I do. Do not, however, concoct an ersatz one by suspending a metal colander over a stockpot — this oft-suggested method seldom produces satisfactory results.

⅔ cup dried chickpeas
3 tablespoons olive oil
2 pounds lean boneless lamb
  shoulder
½ cup chopped white onions
5 cups boiling water
3 tablespoons fresh lemon juice
½ cup chopped ripe tomatoes
½ teaspoon cinnamon
¼ teaspoon freshly grated
  nutmeg

1 bay leaf
2 teaspoons crushed dried mint
1 scant teaspoon salt (or to taste)
¼ teaspoon freshly ground black
  pepper
4 medium-sized carrots
3 small turnips
2 cups *couscous*
3 small zucchini
2 Italian sweet peppers

Steps

1. Soak the chickpeas overnight in four times their volume of water in a noncorrosible bowl.
2. Heat the olive oil in a heavy-bottomed 5- to 7-quart pot.
3. Cut the lamb into 1-inch cubes. Brown them (in batches, if necessary) on all sides over moderate heat. Transfer the meat to a warm platter.
4. Reduce the temperature to low and sauté the onions for 2 minutes, stirring frequently.
5. Add the lamb, boiling water, lemon juice, tomatoes, cinnamon, nutmeg, bay leaf, mint, salt, and pepper. Stir, cover, and simmer the mixture for 20 minutes.
6. Drain the chickpeas and stir them into the lamb mixture. Simmer the ingredients, covered, for 45 minutes.

7. Begin this step 5 minutes before step 6 is completed. Peel the carrots and turnips. Cut the carrots into ¾-inch-long segments and the turnips into ¾-inch cubes. When step 6 is completed, stir these ingredients into the pot containing the lamb. Simmer, covered, for 15 minutes.

8. Begin this step as soon as the carrots and turnips start simmering in step 7. Put the *couscous* pellets in a 2- to 3-quart pan. Pour cold tap water into the pan until it reaches a depth of 1 inch above the pellets. Soak the pellets for 10 minutes.

9. Pour the *couscous* into a sieve, discarding the water. Return the *couscous* to its soaking pan. Slowly strain two cups of the broth from the large pot into the *couscous*. Bring this mixture to a simmer. Cover, and cook for 5 minutes over low heat.

10. Slice the zucchini into ¾-inch cubes and the peppers into ¼-inch-thick rings. When step 7 is completed, stir in both ingredients and simmer the mixture, covered, for 10 minutes.

11. It should be time to turn off the heat under the simmering *couscous* pellets as soon as the zucchini-and-pepper mixture starts simmering in step 10. Fluff the pellets, cover the pan, and let it stand for 8 minutes. Then pour off any remaining liquid.

12. Mound the *couscous* pellets in the center of a warm, large serving platter. Using a slotted spoon, remove the meat and vegetables from the pot and neatly arrange them around the mound.

Additional Keys to Success

Trim all the surface fat off the lamb chunks. ¶ Do not let the liquid boil in steps 5, 6, 7, and 10. If it does, the lamb will toughen. ¶ If you are using coarse- as opposed to medium-grind *couscous* pellets, extend the cooking time by 5 minutes.

Serving Suggestions and Affinities

Arrange a few parsley sprigs around the edge of the mound. ¶ Traditionally, *couscous* is accompanied by a hot sauce called *hrisa* (or *harissa*). You can prepare it at home by combining ¼ cup finely minced chili peppers with 1 tablespoon each of lemon juice, olive oil, and broth from the lamb pot. ¶ Serve some of the strained broth in a sauceboat. Pour it over the *couscous* pellets if they lose some of their moisture at the table. ¶ In North Africa, *couscous* is customarily eaten with the right hand, using the thumb and first two fingers. Sometimes the meat, vegetables, and *couscous* pellets are scooped up with pieces of pita or other flat bread. ¶ The best alcoholic beverage accompaniment is beer or a hearty red wine (Muslims, of course, abstain from alcohol). ¶ Follow the *couscous* with a dessert course of fresh fruits. End the meal with glasses of hot mint tea.

Variations on a Theme

Couscous is also made with chicken, mutton, kid, beef, and seafood — alone or combined. Vegetable *couscous* also exists. ¶ Some cooks add flavoring ingredients such as saffron, garlic, and ginger to the pot.

Mail-Order Sources

Couscous and *hrisa* (or *harissa*) are available through the mail from Karnig Tashjian, 380 Third Avenue, New York, New York 10016 (212-683-8458). Saffron and ginger are available from H. Roth & Son, 1577 First Avenue, New York, New York 10028 (212-734-1110).

◄§ Csirke Paprikás   *Serves 4*
(CHEER-kah PAH-pree-kash)

The Great Plain of Hungary is laced with venerable rivers, including the mighty Danube. On its fertile soil farmers harvest wheat, corn, potatoes, cabbage, and — the trademark of Hungarian cuisine — paprika. This finely crushed red pepper lends both flavor and hue to food, which is fine with the Hungarians, as they like hearty and colorful dishes.

I've tasted various paprikas of the world, including those from Spain, and have to admit that the Hungarians' spice has a certain subtle piquancy that makes it the standard against which all other paprikas should be judged. Hungarian paprika comes in three styles: "sweet," "medium," and "hot." Sweet is the preferred version for most dishes, including *csirke paprikás,* or, as we know it, chicken paprika.

Chicken paprika is one of the world's most widely cooked dishes. I've seen it offered on menus throughout Europe and America, and even in Tokyo and Singapore. Sadly, the chicken paprika cooked in those lands bears scant resemblance, in terms of quality and taste, to the ones I sampled in rural areas of Hungary. Prepare this Hungarian peasant recipe and you, too, will notice the difference.

1 3-pound chicken
¼ cup chopped chicken fat
½ cup sliced white onions
Heaping ½ teaspoon salt (or to taste)
2 tablespoons sweet paprika

¼ cup chopped peeled tomato
1 Italian sweet pepper cut into julienne strips
1 tablespoon flour
½ cup sour cream

Steps

1. Cut the chicken into eight pieces (if the butcher has not already done so).
2. Place the neck, gizzard, and heart in a saucepan containing 1¼ cups of cold water. (Save the liver for another use.) Bring to a low boil and cook, uncovered, for 30 minutes, or until the liquid is reduced to about ⅓ cup. Turn the neck over halfway through the cooking period.
3. Render the chicken fat in a heavy 3- to 4-quart casserole over medium heat. Brown the chicken (in batches, if necessary) for a total of about 3 minutes per piece, and remove the pieces to a warm platter.
4. Sauté the onions in the casserole over low to medium heat for about 2 minutes.
5. Strain the broth from step 2 and pour it into the casserole.
6. Stir the salt, paprika, tomato, and sweet pepper into the onion mixture. Return the drumsticks to the pot and coat them with the sauce. Cover, and simmer the preparation for 5 minutes.
7. Return the remaining chicken to the pot and simmer, covered, for 20 to 25 minutes.
8. Transfer the chicken to a warm serving bowl.
9. Reduce the heat to a low simmer.
10. Blend the flour into the sour cream thoroughly. Slowly add this mixture to the pot, stirring constantly.
11. Cook the sauce for about 3 to 5 minutes, until it begins to thicken.
12. Pour the sauce over the chicken. Serve the *csirke paprikás* immediately.

Additional Keys to Success

Use the chicken fat from the bird's cavity. If there is none, substitute 2 tablespoons of lard or butter. ¶ Never add (as some recipes specify) the paprika to the hot fat, as that procedure guarantees that the paprika will develop a bitter off-flavor. ¶ A tomato can be peeled easily if it is first submerged in boiling water for 30 to 60 seconds (depending on its variety) and then quickly immersed in cold tap water. ¶ If you do not have fresh, vine-ripened tomatoes, use a good brand of canned Italian plum tomatoes. ¶ The chicken will toughen if you cook it at a higher heat or for a longer period than is suggested. ¶ If the sour cream cooks at too high a heat or for too long, it may curdle.

Serving Suggestions and Affinities

Buttered noodles — especially *csipetke* or *spaetzle* — are traditional accompaniments to *csirke paprikás*. Rice or dumplings are other worthy side dishes. ¶ Serve the widely available Hungarian red wine Egri Bikaver (literally, "bull's blood").

Variations on a Theme

Many Hungarian households substitute veal for the chicken. In this case, a veal broth is used and the meat is simmered for about an hour.

Mail-Order Source

Sweet paprika, *csipetke,* and *spaetzle* are available through the mail from Paprikás Weiss, 1546 Second Avenue, New York, New York 10028 (212-288-6117).

❧ Curried Kid   *Serves 4*

Jamaica has an exciting variety of culinary specialties, including its own version of pepper pot, a savory soup-stew of pork or beef and vegetables. Among the other popular dishes are red pea soup (the "pea" is the red kidney bean), stamp and go (salt cod fritters) and salt cod akee (made with the same seafood staple as in stamp and go, but this time cooked with the yellow flesh of the akee fruit).

The one dish that I most closely associate with Jamaica, however, is curried kid. When a Jamaican peasant family cooks a dinner for a special occasion, the menu is more likely to feature this braised dish than any other mainstay of the varied local gastronomic repertoire.

I was served curried kid by a farm family who lived in the foothills of the east–west-central mountain range that cuts Jamaica in half. It was much too humid and hot on that particular Sunday afternoon to eat indoors, so we ate at the back-yard table. Banana trees, heavy with maturing fruit, and a natural "fence" of bamboo stalks, soaring thirty feet toward the tropical sky, shaded us from the intense rays of the sun.

I can't duplicate that lovely setting, but I did bring the recipe home with me. Kid meat may be hard to come by in some sections of the United States, but it is worth searching for a butcher who will order it for you.

1½ pounds lean, boneless kid	2 teaspoons curry powder
1½ tablespoons lard	¼ cup chopped fresh chili pepper
⅔ cup chopped onions	½ teaspoon salt (or to taste)
1 teaspoon minced fresh ginger	½ cup boiling water
1 teaspoon minced garlic	2 tablespoons vinegar

Steps

1. Cut the kid into 1-inch cubes. Trim off any exterior fat or gristle.
2. Melt the lard in a heavy-bottomed 4- to 5-quart casserole over moderate to high heat.
3. Brown the meat (in batches, if necessary) on all sides in the hot fat. Transfer the pieces to a warm platter.
4. Reduce the heat to low to moderate. Sauté the onions for 2 minutes, stirring frequently. Add the ginger and garlic. Sauté the mixture for 1 minute, stirring constantly.
5. Stir the curry powder, chili pepper, and salt into the mixture. As soon as the ingredients are blended, stir in the water and vinegar.
6. Return the meat to the casserole. Bring the liquid to a gentle simmer, stir the ingredients, cover the pot, and cook the preparation over very low heat for 1½ hours. Turn and coat the meat pieces every half-hour. Serve promptly.

Additional Keys to Success

Use the meat from the shoulder or the leg. The former will be more flavorful and the latter more tender. ¶ If the pan is crowded in step 3, the meat will be steaming in its own juices rather than browning in the fat. Unless you use a very wide-bottomed pot, brown the meat in batches. ¶ Do not let the onion or garlic cook at too high a heat or for too long in step 4. Otherwise, it will brown and become bitter. ¶ When cutting the chili pepper, be careful not to touch your eyes. Wash the knife blade and work surface as well as your hands when you have completed the cutting task. ¶ Use a fresh, top-quality brand of curry powder. Even better, blend your own curry mixture. ¶ The prompt addition of the liquid in step 5 is necessary to prevent the spices from scorching and therefore becoming bitter in the hot oil. ¶ If the liquid boils in step 6, the meat will shrink and toughen.

Serving Suggestions and Affinities

Plain rice is the most popular starch accompaniment. Mound the rice in a warm, shallow serving bowl; then form a crater in its center. Spoon the curried kid, sauce and all, into this hollow. ¶ A full-flavored green vegetable, such as spinach, is a fitting side dish. ¶ Because of the curry and chili, wine is not suitable to serve with this dish. Beer is.

Variations on a Theme

Marinate the meat cubes overnight in the vinegar. Pat them dry before browning them. Add the marinade to the pot in step 5. ¶ In place of all or part of the water, use an unseasoned stock made from kid, veal, or chicken bones. ¶ Substitute goat for the kid. Because that meat comes from an older animal, it will have a more pronounced flavor and will require extra cooking time.

Mail-Order Source

Fresh ginger and curry powder are available through the mail from H. Roth & Son, 1577 First Avenue, New York, New York 10028 (212-734-1110).

✒️ Fiskepudding

(FEEZ-keh-POOD-ding)

Serves 6

Norway, scarcely larger than Wyoming, boasts a shoreline measuring an estimated 12,000 miles, a distance equaling approximately half the circumference of the earth. Making this statistic possible are Norway's plentiful islands and fjords.

The awesome sheer-sided fjords penetrate upwards of a hundred miles into Norway's pine-clad mountainous mainland. Narrow, precipitous branches of these fjords further probe the land, as if exploring the rugged yet placid terrain ruled a thousand years ago by the venturesome Vikings.

As our coastal steamship silently made its way up a fjord on a late spring morning, I spotted high above me cliff-hanging glaciers and farmsteads defying the laws of gravity. At eye level were fishing villages tucked into sheltered coves.

Because these were the exhilarating days before the summer solstice, the villages were alive with activity. Residents were making the most of the twenty-four-hour days in this land of the midnight sun. Within six months the sun would hardly, if ever, rise above the horizon, leaving the sky to nature's most exciting light show, the aurora borealis.

I saw villagers preserving freshly caught cod by festooning the fillets on taut ropes, where they would dry for several weeks in the bright rays of the sun. But one of the fish went directly from the boat to the kitchen of my host for making the light and snowy fish mousse called *fiskepudding*.

1 teaspoon unsalted butter
3 tablespoons unseasoned bread
  crumbs
1½ pounds skinned and boned
  cod
⅔ teaspoon salt (or to taste)

⅛ teaspoon freshly ground black
  pepper
⅛ teaspoon ground mace
⅛ teaspoon ground cardamom
1½ tablespoons cornstarch
½ cup light cream
1 cup heavy cream

Steps

1. Preheat the oven to 350° F. Also, bring about 1 quart of water to a boil.
2. Rub the interior of a 1- to 1½-quart mold thoroughly with the butter. Sprinkle with the bread crumbs. Shake out any excess crumbs.
3. Cut the fish into chunks and place them in a food processor equipped with the steel blade. Add the salt, pepper, mace, cardamom, and cornstarch. Blend the ingredients at high speed as you slowly add the creams. Continue blending until the purée is smooth and fluffy.
4. Pour the purée into the mold. Smooth the surface of the purée with a spatula. Cover the top of the mold with aluminum foil and seal it well.
5. Put the mold inside a wider but shallower baking pan and place both in the middle of the oven. Pour the boiling water into the pan to a depth of about ¾ inch.
6. Bake the preparation for 50 to 60 minutes, or until a knife blade inserted into the center of the *fiskepudding* comes out clean.
7. Remove the baking pan from the oven. Take the mold out of the pan and let it stand for about 5 minutes.
8. Unmold the *fiskepudding:* First, pour off any liquid in the mold. Place a warm serving platter over the mold. Quickly but carefully invert the mold and platter simultaneously. Tap the mold and remove it. Use paper towels to soak up any liquid that drains out of the *fiskepudding* onto the platter. Serve immediately.

Additional Keys to Success

The fish must be unequivocally fresh. ¶ Any shape mold, including a soufflé dish or loaf pan, is adequate, but a ring-shaped mold is best. ¶ The traditional method of preparing *fiskepudding* is by hand. However, because food processors and blenders produce a lighter product better and faster, it seems silly nowadays to employ the old, laborious hand method. ¶ If your food processor doesn't have a large bowl, or if you have a blender, divide the ingredients and prepare the purée in several batches. ¶ Settle the purée by lightly striking the bottom of the mold several times on a counter top. ¶ If the water in the pan boils in step 6, your *fiskepudding* may have as many holes as a Swiss cheese. Should the water begin to boil, reduce the oven temperature by about 25° F.

Serving Suggestions and Affinities

Serve the *fiskepudding* with melted butter flavored with dill and lemon juice. Or, prepare a shrimp-, lobster-, caper-, or tomato-based sauce. ¶ Ring the unmolded *fiskepudding* with parsley sprigs, or stick a single sprig of parsley tree-style into the top of the *fiskepudding*. ¶ An ideal beverage for *fiskepudding* is a dry, medium-bodied California Chardonnay. Beer, though, is a more traditional accompaniment.

Variations on a Theme

Substitute potato flour for the cornstarch. ¶ Substitute another firm-textured, nonoily fish such as haddock or halibut.

Leftovers

Prepare open-faced sandwiches with slices of cold *fiskepudding*. ¶ Bread slabs of *fiskepudding* and pan-fry them in butter.

Mail-Order Source

Ground mace and ground cardamom are available through the mail from H. Roth & Son, 1577 First Avenue, New York, New York 10028 (212-734-1110).

◄§ Ground Nut Stew   *Serves 4*

I've tasted ground nut (peanut) stew up and down West Africa, from Gabon in the south to Senegal in the north. Ground nut stew is the generic name used in former British colonies, such as Ghana and Nigeria. Even within those nations the appellation seems to change within a day's drive — many a local tribe still prefers to call the dish by a unique name its ancestors coined centuries ago, and if villagers down the river give the dish another title, that's their problem.

Recipes change, too, from one hut to the next. The one indispensable ingredient is the peanut. Depending on custom and availability, the cook can stir into the pot almost any kind of meat — chicken or fish, for instance — or she can make ground nut stew a strictly vegetarian affair. The latter approach is the norm for the poorest West African peasants, who can't afford the luxury of meat.

The chicken ground nut stew I savored in a small Nigerian village was accompanied by *fufu*, made from cooked cassava. *Fufu* — which can also be prepared from millet, plantains, or yams — is traditionally eaten in a sensuous way. Using your fingers, you scoop up some of the pasty *fufu*, mold it into a 1-inch ball, dip it into the liquid in the ground nut stew, pop it into your mouth, and slowly swallow it.

1 3-pound chicken
3 tablespoons peanut oil
1 cup chopped shallots
2 cups unseasoned chicken stock
  (see page 195)
1 cup chopped tomatoes
2 tablespoons fresh lemon juice

⅔ cup freshly ground shelled,
  skinned, and roasted peanuts
½ teaspoon thyme
Heaping ½ teaspoon salt (or to
  taste)
¼ cup chopped fresh chili pepper
12 medium-sized okra
4 hard-cooked eggs, peeled

Steps

1. Cut the chicken into twelve pieces (if your butcher has not already done so).
2. Heat the oil in a thick, wide-bottomed 4- to 6-quart pot over moderate heat.
3. In batches, brown the chicken pieces on all sides. Transfer them to a warm platter and partially cover them with aluminum foil.
4. Reduce the heat to low and sauté the shallots for 2 minutes (add 1 extra teaspoon of oil, if necessary). Stir frequently.
5. Stir in the chicken stock, tomatoes, and lemon juice. Raise the heat. Bring the mixture to a boil, stirring occasionally.
6. Blend ½ cup of the stock into the ground peanuts. Stir the peanut mixture into the pot.
7. Stir in the thyme, salt, and chili pepper. Return the chicken to the pot. Bring the preparation to a simmer. Reduce the heat to low. Cover, and simmer the preparation for 35 minutes.
8. Trim off the stems and tips of the okra and slice them into ½-

inch-long chunks. Stir them into the pot. Cover, and simmer for 4 to 8 minutes (young okra take the least time).

9. Partially submerge the eggs in the preparation. Cover and continue cooking the mixture for another 3 minutes. Serve immediately.

Additional Keys to Success

If vine-ripened tomatoes are unavailable, substitute a good brand of canned imported Italian tomatoes. Drain them before chopping. ¶ If necessary, substitute commercial peanut butter for the ground peanuts. ¶ Increase or decrease the quantity of chili pepper to match your immunity to the burning effects of the capsicum, but do not reduce the amount too much because this dish is characteristically hot. ¶ When preparing chilies, do not touch your eyes with your hands. Wash both the knife blade and cutting surface as soon as you finish the cutting task. ¶ If fresh chili peppers are unavailable, substitute 1 teaspoon of dried red pepper (cayenne).

Serving Suggestions and Affinities

Serve a medley of accompaniments, such as *fufu*, baby eggplants, cubed pineapple, fried plantains, orange sections, raw onion rings, shredded coconut, sliced papaya, steamed rice, tomato wedges, unsalted roasted peanuts, and whole bananas. Also serve one or two green-vegetable side dishes.

Variations on a Theme

If it's available, substitute palm nut oil for the peanut oil. ¶ Make your peanut stew with beef, fish, shrimp, lamb, or kid rather than poultry. Or, mix two or more main ingredients, shrimp and chicken, for example. ¶ Eliminate the meat and prepare a peanut stew featuring one or more green vegetables.

⋖ξ Hoppel Poppel   *Serves 2*
(HOP-pel POP'l)

Some military draftees spend their tour of duty in remote Goose Bay, Labrador, or, even worse, in a combat zone. In the 1950s I was more fortunate. My assigned base was in the middle of a cluster of farms near a small village twenty miles outside the turreted medieval city of Nürnberg, West Germany. The local farmers and burghers weren't ordinary folk; they shared a deep love and respect for their hearty German food.

Because I frequented the gasthauses and rathskellers, the two focal points of social life in this and most other German villages, I met many of the farmers. Over endless beers, we talked and talked. As soon as they learned of my keen interest in their regional cuisine, it wasn't long before I was being invited to their homes to meet their families and learn about their cooking traditions.

The meals I ate (and sometimes helped to prepare) varied from the simple to the elaborate. In the quick-and-easy-dish department, none tasted better than *hoppel poppel,* which is a disk-shaped omelet enlivened with onions, herbs, and leftover meat and potatoes. The farmer's wife who taught me how to make it usually served it as the principal dish for a casual midweek meal, but it also seems ideal for an American Sunday brunch.

½ cup diced leftover lean pork
3 large eggs
4 tablespoons unsalted butter
¼ cup chopped white onions
⅔ cup diced leftover peeled
   boiled potatoes

1 tablespoon heavy cream
½ teaspoon chopped fresh dill
¼ teaspoon salt (or to taste)
⅛ teaspoon freshly ground black
   pepper
2 dill sprigs

Steps

1. Remove the pork and eggs from the refrigerator approximately 45 minutes before proceeding to the next steps.
2. Melt the butter in a medium-sized or large skillet over low to moderate heat. Add the onions and sauté them for about 1 minute, stirring constantly.
3. Add the potatoes and sauté for about 3 minutes. Stir frequently.
4. Add the pork and sauté for about 3 minutes. Stir frequently.
5. Break the eggs in a bowl and add to them the cream, chopped dill, salt, and pepper. Beat this mixture as you would for a standard omelet.
6. Pour the egg mixture over the potatoes, meat, and onions in the

skillet. Cover the skillet, reduce the heat to low, and cook the preparation for about 5 minutes, or until the eggs have set.

7. Slide the *hoppel poppel* onto a warm plate. Place on top of this plate another warm plate of the same size. Securely hold the plates together and quickly but carefully invert them so that the more attractive browned side of the *hoppel poppel* is face up.

8. Garnish the *hoppel poppel* with the dill sprigs. Cut it at the table into pizza-style wedges. Serve immediately.

Additional Keys to Success

Unless you remove the potatoes, pork, and eggs from the refrigerator early, your *hoppel poppel* will not be light and fluffy. ¶ If you don't have fresh dill for step 5, substitute 1 teaspoon chopped fresh parsley, preferably the Italian variety. ¶ To help keep the eggs from sticking to the pan, periodically jerk the skillet back and forth. ¶ After sliding the *hoppel poppel* from the skillet to the plate, use paper towels to soak up any butter puddles. Otherwise, butter may drip out between the two plates when you invert them.

Serving Suggestions and Affinities

Accompany *hoppel poppel* with a green salad, crusty white bread, cheese, and a bowl of fresh fruits.

Variations on a Theme

Sprinkle the browned side of your *hoppel poppel* with grated cheese and briefly run it under the broiler. ¶ Substitute leftover chicken, turkey, beef, veal, ham, shrimp, crab meat, or firm-fleshed fish for the pork. Or, use bacon (in which case you won't need the butter as a cooking fat). ¶ Scramble your *hoppel poppel* rather than prepare it as an omelet.

ᶓ Huachinango a la Veracruzano   *Serves 3 to 4*
(wah-chee-NAHN-go ah lah vehr-ah-crew-THAH-no)

Red snapper has always been one of my favorite fishes. I've enjoyed this subtly flavored food cooked in a number of tempting ways, but never has it tasted better than when prepared as *huachinango a la veracruzano.*

I came across this recipe in a small village in the hills of the state of Veracruz, Mexico. As I was eating this version of *huachinango a la veracruzano,* two pleasant and captivating scents competed for my attention. One was the wafting aroma of the baked red snapper in its spicy tomato sauce. The other was the luscious perfume of the gardenias growing randomly on the latticework of the nearby terrace.

Beyond the garden wall I could see the village bathed in the light of the full moon. The houses, which sported red tile roofs and white and pastel-hued stucco walls, were connected by a jumble of narrow cobblestone alleys. Potted flowers, moving ever so slightly in the fresh evening breeze, sat as silent beauty on window ledges and wooden balconies. It was a night for dining.

1 2½- to 3½-pound dressed, whole red snapper
2 tablespoons lime juice
2 tablespoons vegetable oil
½ cup thinly sliced white onions
1 teaspoon minced garlic

1 cup chopped vine-ripened tomatoes
2 tablespoons chopped fresh coriander
1 teaspoon chopped fresh chili pepper
Pinch of cinnamon
¼ teaspoon salt

Steps

1. Preheat oven to 350° F.
2. Rub the fish (including its stomach cavity) with 1 tablespoon of the lime juice. Set the fish aside for step 5.
3. Heat the oil in a medium-sized, heavy-bottomed saucepan over low to moderate heat. Sauté the onions for 1 minute, stirring frequently. Add the garlic and sauté the mixture for 1 minute, stirring constantly.

4. Stir in the tomatoes, coriander, chili, salt, and the remaining 1 tablespoon of lime juice. Simmer the sauce for 30 minutes.

5. Place the fish in a greased, shallow baking pan. Spread 2 tablespoons of the sauce in the cavity of the fish. Pour the remaining sauce over the fish. Bake the fish for 12 to 20 minutes, depending on its thickness. Turn the fish over and spoon some of the sauce on top of the fish. Bake the fish for another 8 to 12 minutes, or until the flesh at its thickest part flakes when pierced and prodded with the tines of a fork. Promptly transfer the fish to a warm serving platter and pour the sauce over the fish (or leave the fish and its sauce in the baking dish). Serve immediately.

Additional Keys to Success

If red snapper is unavailable, use another nonoily ocean fish, such as pompano or sea bass. Of course, since *huachinango* means red snapper, you'll have to rename your dish. ❡ Do not cut off the head and tail before cooking the fish. Otherwise, the flesh will lose too much of its flavorful juice during the baking process. ❡ The onions and garlic will burn and therefore develop a sharp, bitter taste if they are cooked over too high heat or for too long in step 3. ❡ If fresh vine-ripened tomatoes are unavailable, substitute a good brand of canned Italian plum tomatoes. Drain before using. ❡ Use another herb if fresh coriander is unavailable. Remember, a dried herb generally has more than twice the flavoring power of an equivalent volume of the fresh herb. ❡ Chili must be handled with caution. Do not rub your eyes after touching the cut chili. Thoroughly wash the knife blade and work surface when the cutting task is completed. ❡ Unless the sauce cooks for 30 minutes in step 4, the finished sauce in step 5 will be too watery. ❡ Avoid overcooking the fish so that it does not develop a mushy texture.

Serving Suggestions and Affinities

Sprinkle chopped fresh coriander or parsley on top of the cooked *huachinango a la veracruzano.* ❡ Ring the fish with lime slices or wedges. ❡ Serve a green vegetable as a side dish as well as either plain rice, boiled new potatoes, or warmed tortillas. ❡ Open a dry, semiassertive white wine such as an Orvieto. Beer is another fine beverage accompaniment.

Variations on a Theme

Add chopped sweet peppers, olives, and/or capers to the sauce.
§ Rather than using a whole fish, buy fish fillets. In this case, briefly
sauté the fillets for about a minute per side before you place them
in the baking pan. Reduce the baking time. There is no need to
turn the fish during the baking period.

☙ Huevos Rancheros   *Serves 2*
(WEH-vos rahn-CHEH-rohs)

I lived half a year of my childhood in San Miguel de Allende, a peaceful
Mexican town built on the slope of a hill overlooking an expansive
valley. At that time, San Miguel wasn't the tourist mecca it is today,
but the first wave of expatriate artists — with palettes and suitcases
in hand — was already arriving in appreciable numbers.

Their "Motif Number One" consisted of the numerous Spanish
Colonial buildings that lined the quaint and winding cobblestone
streets. They also took time to dab on their canvases the image of
my favorite local edifice: a somewhat eccentric pink-stone church stee-
ple designed by an Indian architect who had used etchings of French
cathedrals as his reference material. The result of his composition
is described as Mexican Gothic.

I also enjoyed San Miguel's countryside. My family lived in a
home near the outskirts of San Miguel and frequently took horseback
rides through the nearby hills, exploring ranches, farms, and wide-
open country. It was in this environment that I was introduced to
the spicy country-style eggs called *huevos rancheros.*

4 tablespoons lard	1 medium-sized fresh green chili
¼ cup thinly sliced white onions	pepper cut into julienne strips
1 teaspoon minced garlic	¼ teaspoon ground cumin
⅔ cup chopped vine-ripened tomatoes	⅛ teaspoon salt (or to taste)
	2 corn tortillas
	2 large eggs

Steps

1. Preheat the oven to 200° F.
2. Melt 1 tablespoon of the lard in a thick-bottomed 1- to 2-quart saucepan over low to moderate heat.
3. Sauté the onions for 2 minutes, stirring frequently. Add the garlic and sauté the mixture for 1 minute, stirring constantly.
4. Stir in the tomatoes, chili, cumin, and salt. Simmer the sauce, uncovered, for 20 minutes, stirring frequently.
5. Melt the remaining lard in a heavy-bottomed, medium-sized skillet over moderate heat. Fry a tortilla in the fat for approximately 30 seconds per side. Transfer it to paper towels, pat it dry, and place it in the preheated oven. Prepare the other tortilla in the same fashion.
6. Reduce the heat in the skillet to low and wait a couple of minutes for the fat to cool slightly. Fry one of the eggs in the fat until the whites are just set. Transfer the egg to a warm platter, cover it with foil, and fry the second egg in the same manner.
7. Place a tortilla on each of two warm dinner plates. Place a fried egg on each tortilla. Spoon the sauce over the eggs. Serve promptly.

Additional Keys to Success

Substitute vegetable oil (or a combination of 3 tablespoons vegetable oil and 1 tablespoon butter) for the lard if the latter is unavailable. ¶ If vine-ripened tomatoes are unavailable, use a good brand of imported plum tomatoes. ¶ Do not sauté the onions and garlic at too high a heat or for too long. Otherwise, they will burn and develop a bitter taste. ¶ When handling the chili peppers, do not touch your eyes. Wash the knife blade and work surface thoroughly when you have completed the cutting task. ¶ If you want your sauce to be hotter, add the chili seeds. ¶ Do not overcook the tortillas in step 5 or they will become crisp and brittle. ¶ In step 6, the fat must not be too hot or the egg whites will develop a rubbery texture. ¶ Do not let the egg yolks cook beyond the semirunny stage. Otherwise, the yolk won't be able to blend with the tomato sauce when the diner cuts into the *huevos rancheros.*

Serving Suggestions and Affinities

Huevos rancheros are usually eaten for breakfast or brunch. ¶ Garnish your dish with sliced fresh avocado. ⁋ Accompany your *huevos rancheros* with side dishes of refried beans, *queso blanco* or another soft and mild cheese, whole chili peppers, sausage, and fresh tortillas. ⁋ Serve hot chocolate.

Variations on a Theme

Experiment with different flavoring agents for the tomato sauce — fresh coriander leaves, for instance. ⁋ Prepare and serve two eggs on top of each tortilla. In this case, fry the eggs together so that they form the necessary round shape. ⁋ Use poached or scrambled rather than fried eggs. ⁋ Just before you serve your *huevos rancheros*, sprinkle them with some melting cheese and run the (heat-proof) platter briefly under the broiler. ⁋ Rather than spooning the sauce over the middle of the egg, add it around the circumference of the egg. ⁋ Instead of presenting the *huevos rancheros* on dinner plates, bring them to the table on a large warm serving platter.

Mail-Order Source

Ground cumin is available through the mail from H. Roth & Son, 1577 First Avenue, New York, New York 10028 (212-734-1110).

⋑ Hung Shao Chu Jou *Serves 4 to 6*
(HUNG ZHOW ZHEW JEW)

Red-cooked dishes are popular in and around Shanghai. This term, of course, refers not to the political persuasion of the cook but to the reddish color imparted to a meat as it slowly braises in a generous amount of soy sauce.

I enjoyed a particularly savory red-cooked dish made with pork shoulder on one of the countless flat-bottomed wooden craft that ply the rivers and canals of the lower Yangtze Valley. An entire family — two grandparents, a father, mother, and three young children — lived aboard the small boat.

Like millions of other boat people in China, they were born on a vessel and will probably spend the rest of their lives on one. To move to the land is out of the question because they only know how to make a living on the water. Besides, farmland is scarce in a nation of a billion people.

The grandmother prepared the red-cooked pork as her grandmother had — on a small charcoal brazier set on the open deck. By coordinating the cooking times allocated for each dish, she managed to steam long-grained rice and stir-fry a green vegetable on the same portable "stove."

On a normal day, a few small portions of fish would probably be substituted for the pork, but this day was special. Since the pork shoulder did take a big slice out of the family's meager budget, she cooked it with loving care. Here's her recipe, adapted for oven cookery, direct from China to you.

1 4- to 5-pound pork shoulder
½ cup dark soy sauce
½ cup red rice vinegar
⅓ cup thickly sliced scallions

1 teaspoon coarsely chopped garlic
2 teaspoons coarsely chopped fresh ginger
1 whole star anise

Steps

1. Preheat the oven to 300° F.
2. Place the pork shoulder in a heavy-bottomed 5- to 7-quart casserole. Cover the pork with cold tap water.
3. Bring the liquid to a simmer. Cover the pot and simmer the pork for 10 minutes.
4. Pour out the water and replace it with the soy sauce and red rice vinegar. Bring the liquid to a simmer.
5. Stir in the scallions, garlic, ginger, and star anise.
6. Cover the pot and place it in the oven. Cook the preparation for 2 hours (for a 4-pound shoulder) to 2¼ hours (for a 5-pound piece). Turn the meat once at the midpoint of the period.
7. Transfer the pork to a warm plate. Partially cover the pork with foil and let it rest for 15 minutes, or until it is cool enough to handle for step 8.
8. Cut the pork into bite-sized pieces. Discard the bones, fat, and skin (alternatively, you can fry the fat and skin for use as an appetizer).
9. Mound the pork in a warm bowl.
10. Strain the sauce and skim as much of its fat as you can. Pour ⅓

cup of the sauce on top of the pork. (Save the rest of the sauce for another use.) Serve immediately.

Additional Keys to Success

If dark soy sauce is unavailable, substitute light soy sauce. ¶ If you cannot buy red rice vinegar (a sweet product), use white rice vinegar plus 1 tablespoon of sugar. ¶ In place of whole star anise, use ½ teaspoon ground anise seeds or five-spice powder or 1 teaspoon of Pernod. ¶ The liquid must not boil in steps 3, 5, or 6, or the pork will unnecessarily shrink and toughen. ¶ By letting the cooked pork rest in step 7, you let its internal juices settle and redistribute. This minimizes the juice loss when you cut the meat in step 8.

Serving Suggestions and Affinities

The traditional starch staple is rice or steamed buns. ¶ Serve a green vegetable on the side. ¶ A hot clear soup, not tea, is the most popular liquid accompaniment in China. ¶ End the meal with fresh fruit.

Variations on a Theme

Embellish the dish with nuts, mushrooms, and such vegetables as white radishes, turnips, and carrots. ¶ Use another pork cut — hock or tongue, for example. ¶ Brown the meat in hot oil instead of parboiling it. ¶ Red-cooked pork can be prepared in a large wok, in which case it is cooked on top of the stove. ¶ Prepare red-cooked lamb, chicken, or duck.

Mail-Order Sources

Red and white rice vinegars, fresh ginger, five-spice powder, and dark soy sauce are available through the mail from Katagiri & Company, 224 East 59th Street, New York, New York 10022 (212-755-3566). Star anise and ground anise seeds are available from H. Roth & Son, 1577 First Avenue, New York, New York 10028 (212-734-1110).

⊸§ I'a Ota

(EE-ah OH-tah)

Bora-Bora, situated 160 miles northwest of Tahiti, is the fairest tropical island I've ever had the pleasure of exploring. And the fairest day I spent on Bora-Bora was the Sunday I hiked twenty miles around the island.

Above me soared the craggy twin peaks of Mount Oteman and Mount Pahia, 2000-foot-high remnants of the core of an ancient volcano. Along the road paved with crushed coral stood bushes ablaze with colorful hibiscus and bougainvillea, and coconut palms oscillating in the balmy breeze. Always on my left was the turquoise lagoon bounded by a coral reef on the horizon.

Near the end of my walk I met a small group of vacationing Tahitians camping on a solitary beach. One of them was a fisherman by trade, and he invited me to help them prepare *i'a ota,* the marinated raw fish dish of Polynesia. "*Poisson cru* is the famous French version of our native *i'a ota,*" he explained. "*I'a ota* is simpler and, we think, better."

After spearing and netting some tropical fish in the lagoon, we marinated them for several hours. The lime juice in the marinade "cooked" the fish by whitening the flesh and solidifying the protein. Just before serving the preparation, we added — for the sake of color contrast and flavor — some chopped tomatoes, along with coconut milk extracted from the freshly picked fruit of a nearby palm.

Barely ten minutes after we had finished eating the *i'a ota,* the sun began to set. Regrettably, this was the sign for me to take leave of my new-found friends and be on my way to complete the final few miles of my journey. Nightfall comes quickly in the tropics, and the sure, swift veil of darkness would engulf the unlighted road within the hour. My memories of *i'a ota* and that special day will not fade as fast.

½ pound tuna steak
½ pound tilefish or sea bass
½ cup lime juice
½ cup sliced scallions

¼ teaspoon salt (or to taste)
½ cup diced firm tomatoes
¼ cup coconut cream

Steps
1. Skin and bone the fish and slice them into rectangular segments measuring approximately ½ inch by ½ inch by 1½ inches.
2. Place the fish, lime juice, scallions, and salt in a glass or other noncorrosible bowl. Mix the ingredients well but gently. Cover, and refrigerate the preparation for 3 hours.
3. Drain off the excess liquid from the bowl and add the tomatoes and coconut cream. Gently but thoroughly toss the ingredients. Serve the *i'a ota* immediately in chilled glass or porcelain bowls.

Additional Keys to Success
The first rule is to use only very fresh fish obtained from a reliable fishmonger or fisherman. ¶ Never use freshwater fish, as they may contain tapeworms or other parasites (freshwater fish must always be cooked with heat). ¶ You can use most types of ocean fish, including bluefish, cod, haddock, halibut, red snapper, striped bass, swordfish, weakfish, and yellowtail. Ideally, your selection should include one lean fish (tilefish or sea bass, for instance) and one fatty fish (tuna, for example). ¶ The fish will be easier to slice in step 1 if it is well chilled. ¶ Slice the white and at least two inches of the green part of the scallions. ¶ For flavor's sake, select vine-ripened tomatoes.

Serving Suggestions and Affinities
Arrange the *i'a ota* on a single layer of lettuce leaves. ¶ A chilled dry white wine is fine, as long as it doesn't have too many subtleties. A delicate wine will be overpowered by the lime juice.

Variations on a Theme
Use lemon rather than lime juice. ¶ In place of the scallions, use coarsely chopped onions and Italian sweet peppers. ¶ Add such flavoring agents as garlic, chili, mustard, crumbled hard-cooked egg yolks, or freshly ground black pepper. ¶ Include sliced raw octopus or lightly cooked shrimp. ¶ Prepare *i'a ota* with only one type of fish.

Mail-Order Source
Coconut cream is available through the mail from Katagiri & Company, 224 East 59th Street, New York, New York 10022 (212-755-3566).

ᨒᨔ Jollof Rice
(jahl-LAHF)

Serves 3 to 4

The threatening gray morning clouds suddenly released a heavy blanket of rain on the dirt road in Gambia. This tropical downpour stopped almost as abruptly as it began, but the damage was done: My car had slid off the road and was axle deep in mud. Fortunately, my plight was noticed by several women returning from the grassy riverbank with earthenware jugs balanced atop their heads. They smiled and gestured to me to stay put, then disappeared down a footpath with the nonchalant grace that American finishing schools teach for a fee.

Several strapping youths from the nearby village came to my rescue. The only way for me to thank these lads for pushing my car back onto the road was to give them a lift back to their village. They didn't have to tell me its direction, because I was guided by a familiar and mesmerizing West African rhythm emanating from an area beyond a clump of trees. I heard the clockwork thumping sound of women pounding cereal grain with thick poles in hollowed-out cavities of old tree stumps.

As I pulled up to the cluster of squat, wattled huts crowned with freshly thatched roofs, my nose detected a beckoning scent. One of the women was preparing *jollof* rice, a dish so delicious that its popularity has spread throughout most of West Africa.

½ pound boneless lamb shoulder
½ pound boneless chicken breast
  meat
¼ cup fresh lemon juice
3 tablespoons peanut (or other
  vegetable) oil
⅔ cup chopped white onions
1 tablespoon minced fresh
  ginger

2 cups chopped tomatoes
½ cup water
1 teaspoon thyme
1 bay leaf
¼ cup chopped fresh chili
  peppers
½ teaspoon salt (or to taste)
1 cup long-grain white rice
1 parsley sprig

Steps

1. Cut the lamb and chicken into ⅔-inch cubes. Marinate them in the lemon juice in a noncorrosible bowl overnight in the refrigerator.

2. Transfer the meats to paper towels and pat dry. Reserve the marinade for step 5.

3. Heat the oil in a 2- to 3-quart heavy wide-bottomed pot over moderate heat. Briefly brown the meat and transfer it to a warm platter.

4. Reduce the heat to low and sauté the onions for 2 minutes, stirring frequently. Add the ginger and sauté for 1 additional minute, stirring frequently.

5. Stir in the tomatoes, water, reserved marinade, thyme, bay leaf, chili peppers, and salt. Return the lamb to the pot and bring the mixture to a simmer.

6. Cover, and gently simmer the mixture for 30 minutes. Stir in the chicken. Cover, and simmer for another 2 minutes.

7. Stir in the rice. Bring the preparation to a simmer. Cover, and simmer it for 25 minutes without once lifting the lid.

8. Remove the pot from the heat and stir the mixture for a couple of seconds. Quickly cover the pot and let it stand for 5 minutes.

9. Serve the *jollof* rice from the cooking pot or transfer it to a warm serving bowl. Garnish it with the parsley.

Additional Keys to Success

When preparing chili peppers, be careful not to touch your eyes. After chopping the peppers, promptly wash your hands, the knife blade, and the cutting surface. ¶ Do not let the water boil in steps 6 and 7. If it does, the meats will unnecessarily shrink and toughen. ¶ Pour out any excess liquid in the pan after completing step 8.

Serving Suggestions and Affinities

Serve a green vegetable on the side. ¶ You need an assertive wine to stand up to *jollof* rice. Beer is a better choice.

Variations on a Theme

Use other meats, either alone or in combination. ¶ Substitute broth for the water. ¶ Make the dish a one-pot meal by adding a green vegetable, such as okra. ¶ Sauté the rice in oil for several minutes before adding it in step 7. In this case, use 2 tablespoons less water in step 5. Reduce the cooking time by 2 or 3 minutes.

Mail-Order Source

Fresh ginger is available through the mail from H. Roth & Son, 1577 First Avenue, New York, New York 10028 (212-734-1110).

⊷ Karjalan Paisti   *Serves 8*
(KAHR-ee-ah-lahn pie-stee)

My first glimpse of Finland was from the window of an airplane. Below me lay myriad lakes, each reflecting the low-angled rays of the early summer sun, creating a dazzling array of glittering slivers of silver set in a virgin forest that stretched as far as I could see.

The lakes, I soon learned, numbered in the tens of thousands and were teeming with freshwater fish, a mainstay of the traditional Finnish table. Reindeer romped through forests thick with aspen, birch, fir, pine, and spruce trees, and the undergrowth was densely endowed with wild berries and mushrooms waiting for any hungry hiker who happened by. The peaceful silence was interrupted only by the occasional report of a hunter's gun or by the clip of a lumberjack's ax.

During my stay, I visited a small village in the Karelian sector of Finland. The buildings were constructed mainly of logs, as was the onion-domed Orthodox church. One of the families taught me how to prepare the Karelian hot pot. "Avoid the temptation of adding salt or any other seasoning besides dill and allspice," the cook instructed me, "because the unique flavor of the dish is produced when the three meats are cooked unhurriedly together in combination with the natural affinity of dill and allspice." Her definition of a leisurely pace was three hours.

1½ pounds boned beef shoulder	¾ cup water
1½ pounds boned pork shoulder	2 tablespoons chopped fresh dill
1 pound boned lamb shoulder	2 teaspoons ground allspice

Steps
1. Preheat the oven to 275° F.
2. Trim off all the exterior fat on the lamb, but leave some of the exterior fat on the beef and pork. Cut the meat into 1½-inch cubes.

3. Place the water in an oven-proof pot that has a lid. Add and thoroughly blend in the dill and allspice.

4. Add the meat to the pot and thoroughly coat the pieces with the seasoned water.

5. Cover the pot and place it in the oven. Bake for 3 hours. Turn the meat at the midpoint of the cooking process.

6. Serve the meat and sauce separately in warm bowls.

Additional Keys to Success

You must leave on some of the exterior beef and pork fat because it contributes flavor. ¶ If fresh dill is unavailable, substitute 1 teaspoon dried ground dill. ¶ The cooking method for this dish is one that is halfway between stewing and braising. The finished sauce should be full-flavored, so don't add more than the designated quantity of water. ¶ Cooking at a temperature above 275° F will result in unnecessary shrinkage and toughness of the meat. ¶ For flavor's sake, the meat must be eaten with the sauce.

Serving Suggestions and Affinities

Karelians often accompany their *karjalan paisti* with steamed or mashed potatoes and sour rye bread. The sauce is ladled over the meat and potatoes. The rye bread is used to soak up some of the sauce on the plate.

Leftovers

Plan for leftovers because the flavor of *karjalan paisti* develops new dimensions as it rests in the refrigerator.

⋖§ Malu Kiri   *Serves 4*
(mah-loo keer-ee)

Sri Lanka — formerly Ceylon — is an island nation of breathtaking contrasts. Along its coast stretch endless miles of golden white sandy beaches lined with coconut palms swaying in the tropical breeze. Inland are misty mountains and steep hills covered with tea plantations where women, with wicker baskets strapped to their backs, pluck the tenderest of leaves.

Even the climate is varied. While the monsoon season is in full swing on the western side of the island, the eastern shores are bathed in sunshine. Half a year later the climatic conditions reverse themselves. I met one Sri Lankan man who outwitted nature — he kept a home on both sides of the island, and thereby assured himself of perpetual balmy weather.

Sri Lanka (literally, "resplendent land") has been known by a string of names throughout its long history. Until 1972, it was called Ceylon. The early Arab traders referred to it as Serendib, from which springs our word *serendipity*.

It was a serendipitous occasion when I came upon a sleepy fishing village along the western coast just as fishermen were pulling their outriggers onto the beach to unload their catch in front of the milling throng of shoppers. One of the buyers was a woman with two tots in tow. After spending five minutes of friendly haggling with a fishmonger, she exchanged a few coins, picked up the plump fish of her choice from the mat, and dumped it into her basket. I asked her, through an interpreter, how she planned to cook the fish. She answered me by inviting me to share her family's midday meal, and away we went. She prepared *malu kiri*. Like many Singhalese dishes, this delightful specialty is spicy and richly flavored with coconut cream.

2 pounds 1-inch-thick fish steaks
2 tablespoons vegetable oil
½ cup thinly sliced white onions
1 tablespoon minced fresh
   ginger
½ cup coconut cream

2 tablespoons lime juice
2 teaspoons curry powder
¼ cup chopped fresh chili
   peppers
½ teaspoon salt (or to taste)

Steps

1. Skin and bone the fish steaks and cut them into 1-inch cubes. Let them stand in one nontouching layer on a plate at room temperature for 45 minutes.
2. Heat the oil in a large, heavy-bottomed sauté pan or skillet over moderate heat. Sauté the fish on all sides, allowing about 2 minutes per batch. Transfer the fish to a warm platter and partially cover the pieces with aluminum foil.
3. Reduce the heat to low and sauté the onions for 2 minutes, stirring

frequently. Add the ginger and sauté the mixture for 1 minute, stirring frequently.

4. Stir in the coconut cream, lime juice, curry, chili peppers, and salt. Gently simmer the sauce for 3 to 5 minutes, or until it begins to thicken. Stir frequently and scrape off the solid particles that cling to the bottom of the pan.

5. Add the fish, coat the pieces with the sauce, and cover the pan. Cook the preparation for 4 to 6 minutes, or until the fish is done. Transfer the *malu kiri* to a warm serving bowl and serve immediately.

Additional Keys to Success

Select a firm-fleshed fish (halibut, swordfish, or the like). ¶ Use a fresh, top-quality curry powder. Or concoct your own curry powder by blending such ground dried spices as cardamom, chili, cinnamon, cloves, coriander seed, cumin, fennel seeds, fenugreek, mace, nutmeg, and turmeric. ¶ Do not let the preparation boil in steps 4 and 5. Otherwise, the fish cubes will begin to break apart. The same will be true if you overcook the fish or manipulate it roughly during the cutting and cooking stages.

Serving Suggestions and Affinities

Rice is the traditional accompaniment. ¶ Conclude the meal with a bowl of fresh fruits.

Variations on a Theme

Give your *malu kiri* a refreshing twist by adding these popular Sri Lankan flavoring agents: curry leaves, *rampé,* and tamarind. ¶ Substitute shrimp or crab meat for the fish.

Mail-Order Sources

Fresh ginger is available through the mail from Katagiri & Company, 224 East 59th Street, New York, New York 10022 (212-755-3566). Coconut cream, curry powder (and the individual spices that constitute the various blends), and tamarind are available from Kalustyan Orient Expert Trading Corporation, 123 Lexington Avenue, New York, New York 10016 (212-685-3416).

⮑ Matelote à la Bourguignonne   *Serves 4*
(maht-LOHT ah lah bohr-gee-n'YOHN)

One of the most illustrious wine areas, the Côte d'Or in the Burgundy region of France, is less than thirty miles long and — at its broadest point — only a few miles wide. From this small patch of the earth's surface come such majestic wines as Chambertin, Montrachet, and Romanée-Conti. Burgundy, once an independent duchy, is also known for its flinty, white Chablis and its refreshingly light red Beaujolais wines.

Burgundy is the home of world-famous dishes. *Boeuf bourguignonne* and *escargot à la bourguignonne,* for instance, have become menu clichés in stateside French bistros from Maine to California. A Burgundian specialty that has not reached many American eateries is *matelote à la bourguignonne* (also known as *meurette*). It's a freshwater fish stew prepared with red wine.

Fish cooked with red wine? Yes. As long as the wine is young, light-bodied, and low in tannin, this pairing will not assault the palate or break any immutable law of gastronomy. I explore that concept more fully in my book on wine-food affinities, *The Diner's Guide to Wines* (Hawthorn, 1978).

The wife of a vineyard owner in Beaujolais cooked the finest *matelote à la bourguignonne* I've experienced. Adding to the mouth-watering qualities of her offering was the vista from the back-yard table. Spread before me on this bright late-September day were rolling hills blanketed with vines laden with Gamay grapes.

1½ pounds boned and skinned lean freshwater fish
4½ tablespoons unsalted butter
1 tablespoon olive oil
½ cup coarsely chopped shallots
½ teaspoon coarsely chopped garlic
1 cup red wine
4 cups unseasoned freshwater fish stock (see page 196)

1 tablespoon Cognac or marc
1 bay leaf
½ teaspoon thyme
1 teaspoon salt (or to taste)
¼ teaspoon freshly ground black pepper
2 tablespoons chopped fresh parsley
French bread
1½ tablespoons flour

Steps

1. Remove the fish and butter from the refrigerator 20 minutes before starting step 2. Cut the fish into thick, 1½-inch-square pieces and reserve them for step 4.

2. Heat 1 tablespoon of the butter and the oil in a heavy-bottomed, 2½- to 3½-quart pot over low to moderate heat. When the butter has melted, sauté the shallots for 2 minutes. Add the garlic and sauté for 1 minute.

3. Stir in the wine, stock, Cognac, bay leaf, thyme, salt, pepper, and 1 tablespoon of the parsley. Raise the heat and bring the liquid to a rapid boil. Continue to boil for 10 minutes.

4. Add the fish and reduce the heat. Gently simmer the preparation for 5 to 12 minutes, depending on the thickness of the fish pieces.

5. Remove the crust from ten ½-inch-thick slices of French bread and cube the bread. Melt 2 tablespoons of the remaining butter in a large skillet. When the foam begins to subside, add the bread cubes. Toss them in the butter for several minutes, until they are lightly browned.

6. Transfer the fish to a warm serving bowl and cover it.

7. Strain 1½ cups of the cooking liquid into a 1- to 2-quart saucepan and bring it to a simmer. (Discard the remaining stock or reserve it for another purpose, as for a soup base.)

8. Prepare a *beurre manié* by rubbing together the remaining 1½ tablespoons of butter and the flour. Shape the mixture into ¼-inch balls. (If your kitchen is on the warm side, be prepared for very soft *beurre manié* balls.) Add one of these balls to the simmering pot, stir until thoroughly blended into the liquid, and then repeat this operation until all of the *beurre manié* balls have been used.

9. Stir the liquid for 2 minutes after the last *beurre manié* ball has been incorporated.

10. Pour the sauce over the fish. Garnish the top of the *matelote à la bourguignonne* with the croutons and the remaining parsley. Serve at once.

Additional Keys to Success

If you don't remove the butter from the refrigerator ahead of time, it won't be soft enough to prepare the *beurre manié*. ❡ Quickly follow step 2 with step 3 so the garlic does not burn and become bitter. ¶ You can use a light-bodied red wine such as a Mercurey or Givry (or even a regional red Burgundy) for this dish. ¶ If the fish pieces are of unequal thickness, give the thick ones a head start in step 4. ¶ If you add the *beurre manié* balls too quickly, the flour won't blend into the liquid. The same will be true if you don't thoroughly blend the butter and flour into a smooth, creamy paste.

Affinities

Serve a crusty loaf of French bread. ¶ The traditional beverage accompaniment is the same type of wine used in the pot.

Variations on a Theme

Add onions, carrots, leeks, celery, mushrooms, and/or salt pork. ¶ Enrich and thicken the sauce with heavy cream.

◌§ Moules Marinière *Serves 2*

(MOOL mah-ree-n'YAIR)

The world's most famous mussel dish is *moules marinière,* mussels steamed in a shallot- and thyme-flavored wine sauce. Though mollusks make their home in oceans around the globe, the tastiest varieties thrive in cool climates, as found along the western coast of France. Demand for mussels is so great in France that entrepreneurs cultivate them.

I heard an interesting, if unsubstantiated, story from a fisherman's wife about how the art of mussel cultivation began. It was accidentally discovered, she assured me, in the thirteenth century by Patrick Walton, an Irishman shipwrecked on the windswept coastline of France. As part of his survival strategy, he caught low-flying nocturnal birds in a most ingenious fashion: During low tide, he drove poles into the sand and strung fishing nets between them (in my mind's eye, I saw a series of volleyball nets stretched along the beach). Walton soon noticed that young, nourishing mussels were readily affixing themselves to the poles. In time, he gave up his bird-trapping activities in favor of cultivating succulent mussels on netless poles. To this day, the descendants of those mussels are being grown and harvested in the Patrick Walton manner in saltwater pools along the same French shore.

Many of the mussels end up in steaming bowls of *moules marinière* prepared in small fishing villages up and down the French seaboard. Of all the *moules marinière* recipes, the one I learned near Quimper in Brittany should be considered a national culinary treasure of France.

2 dozen small mussels
3 tablespoons plus 1 teaspoon unsalted butter
3 tablespoons chopped shallots
1 cup dry white wine
1 teaspoon thyme

½ teaspoon salt (or to taste)
⅛ teaspoon freshly ground black pepper
1 teaspoon flour
1 tablespoon chopped fresh parsley

Steps

1. Scrub each mussel under warm tap water to remove any slime, sand, or other foreign matter on the shell's outer surface. Scrape off any barnacles with a dull knife.
2. Pull out the beardlike byssus (it's indigestible).
3. Soak the mussels at room temperature for 2 hours in a bowl containing enough cold tap water to cover them by about 3 inches. (This step gives the mussels a chance to suck the water in and out and, in the process, expel some of their internal sand and intestinal waste.) Discard any mussels that float (they're dead or dying).
4. Remove the butter from the refrigerator 30 minutes before beginning step 5. (This will ensure that the butter is sufficiently soft for step 11.)
5. Melt the 3 tablespoons of butter in a wide, heavy-bottomed pot over low to moderate heat. When the foam of the butter begins to subside, add the shallots and sauté them for 1½ minutes.
6. Stir in the wine, thyme, salt, and pepper.
7. Drain and rinse the mussels. Add them to the pot in a single layer when the wine mixture reaches a boil.
8. Cover the pot, reduce the heat to low, and steam the mussels for about 5 to 7 minutes (depending on the size of the mussels), without lifting the lid.

9. Transfer the cooked, opened mussels to warm, shallow bowls. Cover the bowls with aluminum foil. Continue steaming any mussels that have remained closed — but if these mussels do not open in another 2 or 3 minutes, discard them.

10. Strain the pot liquid through a fine sieve into a 1- to 2-quart saucepan and bring it to a gentle simmer.

11. Rub the remaining 1 teaspoon of butter together with the flour. Shape this mixture (*beurre manié*) into ¼-inch balls. Add two or three of these spheres to the simmering sauce, and stir until they are thoroughly blended into the liquid; repeat this operation until all the *beurre manié* has been used.

12. Let the liquid simmer for about 4 minutes, or until the *beurre manié* has slightly thickened the sauce.

13. Pour the sauce over the mussels. Sprinkle the parsley over them, and serve immediately.

Additional Keys to Success

The smaller a mussel is for its variety, the sweeter and more tender it will be. ¶ Discard any mussel with a broken shell — or any that refuses to close when tapped (the mussel is dead or well on its way). ¶ Discard any mussel that feels noticeably light for its size (more than likely, it is dead). ¶ Discard any that feels noticeably heavy for its size or that makes a sound when rattled; it's probably filled with sand. Remember, it takes only one sand-filled mussel to ruin the entire sauce. ¶ If your pot is insufficiently wide, you will have to prepare the *moules marinière* in batches. Or use two pots. ¶ If the water boils vigorously in step 8, the mussels will unnecessarily toughen.

Serving Suggestions and Affinities

As a main course, twenty-four mussels will satisfy two diners of average appetite (but a hungry diner can consume all twenty-four if he relishes mussels). As an appetizer, twenty-four mussels will serve two, three, or possibly four diners. ¶ Serve a basket of crusty French bread for sopping up the sauce. ¶ Uncork a dry white wine. The traditional selections are Muscadet, Sancerre, and Pouilly-Fumé — all from the Loire Valley.

Variations on a Theme

Add ¼ teaspoon chopped garlic 30 seconds before the completion of step 5. ¶ Add a small bay leaf and a sprig of fresh parsley in step 6.

⇜§ Nasi Goreng   *Serves 4*
(nag-SEE go-REHNG)

Bali is a land of superlatives. Wherever I traveled on this tropical Indonesian island, I encountered enchanting sights: peaceful, palm-lined beaches; steaming volcanoes scraping the blue sky; thousands of family-owned temples adorned with offerings of fruit and flowers; secluded villages consisting of clusters of thatched mud-brick huts standing as islands in a sea of verdant rice paddies.

Most of all, I was won over by the Balinese, a people who are immensely generous and attractive, not to mention artistic. The majority of the inhabitants of the isolated villages I visited were dedicated amateurs in at least one art form. Some created exquisite wood or stone carvings; others painted vibrant folk scenes. Yet others (especially the beautiful-eyed young maidens) danced to the bright, tingling rhythms emanating from small ensembles of flutes, xylophones, and bell-like bronze instruments. Their purpose was not art for art's sake, as is often the case in our country, but — as one coffee-plantation owner told me — "to please the many spirits that roam Bali."

The Balinese are culinary artists, too. Their food is full of color and flavor — and it is the hottest in the world (even counting such cuisines as Mexican, Ethiopian, Indian, West African, and Sichuan). Of all the traditional Balinese dishes, the most representative is *nasi goreng* — literally, "fried rice." *Nasi goreng* is more complex than its name suggests, and there are more versions of it than there are sauces in France. This is one of the best.

1½ cups long-grain white rice
½ pound small shrimp
½ pound boneless smoked pork shoulder (or ham)
1 medium-sized boneless chicken breast
5 tablespoons peanut (or other vegetable) oil
2 large eggs
½ cup thickly sliced white onions
1 teaspoon shrimp paste

1 tablespoon soy sauce
1 teaspoon finely minced garlic
½ teaspoon ground cumin
½ teaspoon ground turmeric
½ teaspoon ground coriander seeds
4 tablespoons thinly sliced green chili peppers
¼ cup diced unpeeled cucumbers

Steps

1. Cook the rice (according to package directions) the day before proceeding to step 2. When it has cooled, refrigerate it.
2. Remove the rice from the refrigerator 2 hours before beginning step 3.
3. Shell and devein the shrimp. Cut the smoked pork into ⅓-inch cubes and the chicken breast into ½-inch cubes.
4. Heat 4 tablespoons of the oil in a very large skillet over moderate heat.
5. Beat the eggs. Add them to the hot oil, tilt the skillet so that the eggs form a thin pancake, and fry until the eggs are set. With a slotted spatula, transfer the egg pancake to paper towels; pat it dry. Slice it into long thin shreds and reserve them for step 10.
6. Fry the pork in the hot oil for 1 minute, constantly stirring and tossing it. Add the chicken and fry the mixture for 1 minute, constantly stirring and tossing it. Add the shrimp and fry the mixture for 3 minutes, constantly stirring and tossing it. Transfer the mixture to a warm platter.
7. Add and heat the remaining tablespoon of oil. Reduce the heat to low to moderate. Sauté the onions for 3 minutes, or until they are golden brown. Stir frequently.
8. Add to the onions the shrimp paste, soy sauce, garlic, cumin, turmeric, coriander seeds, and 3 tablespoons of the chili peppers. Quickly stir the mixture. Promptly add the rice. Gently break up any rice clumps. Stir in two thirds of the shrimp, pork, and chicken.

9. Raise the heat to moderate and constantly stir and toss the mixture in the pan for 2 minutes.

10. On a warm serving platter, mound the rice mixture in the shape of a volcano. Artistically garnish it with the shredded egg, arranging the pieces vertically on the slope of the "volcano." Also decorate the mound with the diced cucumbers and the reserved shrimp, pork, chicken, and chili peppers. Serve immediately.

Additional Keys to Success

Do not overcook the rice in step 1 or it will be too mushy to fry properly. ¶ Unless the rice is cooked at least several hours beforehand, it will be insufficiently dry for the frying step. ¶ Remember, the term *chicken breast* indicates the whole breast rather than just the left or right side. ¶ If it is available, use *trasi,* the Indonesian shrimp paste. ¶ If shrimp paste (including *trasi*) is not available, substitute anchovy paste. ¶ Handle the chili peppers with caution. Do not touch your eyes when slicing the peppers. Promptly wash your hands, the knife blade, and the work surface when the cutting task is completed. ¶ Adjust the quantity of chili peppers upward or downward in keeping with your tolerance for chilies. ¶ If you have a wok, use it in place of the skillet.

Serving Suggestions and Affinities

The most popular accompaniment to *nasi goreng* is *krupek,* which are crisp, deep-fried shrimp wafers. ¶ Other possible side dishes include *sambal* (a spicy Indonesian condiment) and roasted peanuts. ¶ Wine is not a suitable choice; beer is.

Variations on a Theme

Garnish the mound with fried eggs rather than with shredded egg pancake. ¶ Other possible garnishes include mushrooms, sweet peppers, and raw or parboiled green vegetables. ¶ Substitute crab or lobster meat for the shrimp. ¶ If your refrigerator contains a leftover meat (including beef or lamb), consider adding it to your creation. ¶ Give your *nasi goreng* added color and pungency with coriander leaves.

Mail-Order Source

Shrimp paste, cumin, turmeric, coriander seeds, *trasi, krupek,* and *sambal* are available through the mail from Mrs. De Wildt, R.D. #3, Bangor, Pennsylvania 18013 (215-588-1042).

⊰ Osso Buco   *Serves 4*
(OHS-soh BOO-koh)

It was the season in the Lombardy region of Italy when brief, bright days and long, lazy nights disrupt the normal flow of daily farm activities. The extra evening hours allowed my host, his wife, and me to linger peacefully at the massive farmhouse table, savoring each bite of *osso buco.*

Osso buco ("hollowed bone") is veal shank braised with onions, wine, and tomatoes and garnished with a piquant mixture of lemon rind, garlic, and parsley. The jewel of this preparation is the bone marrow, which is traditionally extracted with a tiny silver spoon made especially for this gastronomic task. I've heard Italians fancifully call this implement the *agente delle fasse,* "tax collector."

Osso buco is also known in the plural form, *ossi buchi.* By either name, just the thought of this dish is sufficient to set my gastric juices in motion.

Other Lombardian specialties include *vitello tonnato* (simmered boneless leg of veal served cold with a tuna-mayonnaise sauce), *costoletta alla milanese* (Milan's version of Wiener schnitzel), *risotto alla milanese* (saffron-flavored rice), and *minestrone* soup.

4 veal shanks	½ cup unseasoned veal stock
2 tablespoons flour	(see page 195)
3 tablespoons unsalted butter	½ cup chopped peeled tomatoes
1 tablespoon olive oil	1 bay leaf
¾ cup chopped white onions	1 teaspoon rosemary
¼ cup minced carrots	½ teaspoon marjoram
¼ cup chopped celery	½ teaspoon salt (or to taste)
½ cup dry white wine	

¼ teaspoon freshly ground black
  pepper
1 tablespoon grated lemon rind

1 teaspoon finely minced garlic
2 tablespoons chopped fresh
  parsley

Steps

1. Bring the veal shanks to room temperature. Preheat the oven to 300° F.
2. Dredge the veal shanks lightly in the flour.
3. Heat the butter and olive oil in a wide-bottomed 5- to 6-quart casserole over moderate heat.
4. Brown the veal shanks on all sides in the casserole. Transfer the shanks to a warm plate and partially cover them with aluminum foil.
5. Reduce the heat to low and sauté the onions for 2 minutes, stirring frequently. Add the carrots and sauté for 2 minutes, stirring frequently. Add the celery and sauté for 30 seconds, stirring frequently.
6. Stir in the wine, stock, tomatoes, bay leaf, rosemary, marjoram, salt, and pepper. Raise the heat and bring the preparation to a simmer. Continue simmering it for 10 minutes.
7. Return the veal shanks to the casserole. Arrange them upright (ideally, the surface of the bone that contains the largest cross section of marrow should be face upward). Spoon the sauce over the shanks. Cover the pot, place it in the middle of the oven, and cook the preparation for 1½ to 2 hours, depending on the thickness of the veal flesh.
8. Mix the lemon rind, garlic, and parsley. This mixture is called *gremolata.*
9. Transfer the cooked veal shanks to a warm serving platter. Spoon the sauce over the shanks. Sprinkle the preparation with the *gremolata.* Serve promptly.

Additional Keys to Success

For best results, the shank bones should be at least 2 (but preferably 2½) inches long. ¶ For the sake of tenderness, be sure to buy veal — not baby beef — shanks. The color of veal shanks is pale white rather than rosy red. ¶ If you don't have veal stock, substitute chicken stock. ¶ Unless your tomatoes are vine-ripened, use a good brand of canned imported Italian tomatoes; drain the liquid. ¶ When grating the lemon rind, do not cut too deeply into the bitter white pith that underlies the yellow skin.

Serving Suggestions and Affinities

The traditional starch accompaniment to *osso buco* is rice, especially *risotto alla milanese*. Pasta tossed with butter and freshly grated black pepper is a popular alternative. ¶ Serve your *osso buco* on a bed of the rice or pasta. ¶ If you don't have marrow spoons, substitute lobster forks for removing and eating the cooked bone marrow. ¶ Serve a dry, medium-bodied Italian red wine.

Mail-Order Source

Rosemary and marjoram are available through the mail from H. Roth & Son, 1577 First Avenue, New York, New York 10028 (212-734-1110).

⤳ Oyako Donburi   *Serves 4*
(oh-YAH-koh DON-buhr-ee)

One late spring I was the guest of a rice farmer who lived in a thatched dwelling in a small village north of Kyoto, Japan. He owned several paddies, each within walking distance of one another and his home. They were square, barely the size of a badminton court, and enclosed by low-lying mud embankments that served simultaneously as dams, footpaths, and boundary markers.

Rich farming is backbreaking work. The family — husband, wife, and children — must first plant the rice grains in seedling beds. In a month or so, the emerging shoots are replanted by hand in a waiting paddy that has been plowed and flooded with water.

The rice paddies are constantly weeded, and when the grain is mature, they are drained and allowed to dry. The laboring family cuts the plants and threshes the rice by hand. Some of the crop is kept for their use; the rest is sold to pay for the various goods they need to purchase.

On the day of my visit, my host and his family used some of their rice harvest in a dish called *oyako donburi*. *Oyako* means "mother and child," and refers to the chicken and egg in the topping of this version of *donburi*.

Donburi is popular with both peasants and city folk because it is quick and easy to prepare as well as filling and nutritious. It is also a great way for a creative cook to use leftovers.

3 large eggs

2 cups white rice

1½ cups *dashi* (a Japanese soup stock)

¼ cup *mirin* (sweet *sake*)

3 tablespoons soy sauce

1 boned and skinned medium-sized chicken breast

6 medium-sized scallions

Steps

1. Remove the eggs from the refrigerator about 1 hour before starting step 2.
2. Steam the rice, unsalted, according to package directions. Remove from the heat. Fluff the rice. Cover and reserve for step 8.
3. Add the *dashi, mirin,* and soy sauce to a wok or large-sized skillet. Bring the mixture to a boil and cook, uncovered, for 3 minutes.
4. Slice the chicken breast (both halves) across the grain into ¼-inch-thick strips.
5. Slice the scallions into ½-inch-long segments. Use both the white portion and 2 inches of the green.
6. Stir the chicken and scallion pieces into the boiling liquid. Reduce the heat and simmer the preparation, uncovered, for 3 minutes, stirring occasionally.
7. Beat the eggs lightly. Carefully pour them all at once into the center of the simmering mixture. Do not stir the eggs — let them spread out on their own. Cover and gently simmer the preparation for 3 minutes, or until the eggs are lightly set.
8. Divide the rice into four warm individual *donburi* bowls. (If you don't have *donburi* bowls, use deep-sided soup bowls with a capacity of approximately 3 cups.)
9. Divide the solidified egg mixture into four portions. Place them on top of the rice in the individual bowls. Pour over the eggs all the sauce and any remaining chicken and scallion pieces clinging to the wok. Serve immediately.

Additional Keys to Success

Use long- or (preferably) medium-grain rice. ¶ If you don't have *dashi,* substitute unseasoned chicken stock (see page 195). ¶ If you don't have *mirin,* substitute *sake* (or dry sherry) and 1 teaspoon of sugar. ¶ If your pan is not well seasoned, rub its interior with a light coating of vegetable oil before adding the liquid ingredients. This measure helps prevent the eggs from sticking in step 7. ¶ Do not let the liquid boil in steps 6 and 7 or the chicken will shrink and toughen. ¶ Do not let the eggs become fully firm in step 7. They will continue to cook on top of the hot rice.

Serving Suggestions and Affinities

Serve your *donburi* with pickled vegetables. ¶ The liquid accompaniment can be tea, a hot clear soup, or warm *sake.* ¶ *Donburi* is eaten with chopsticks.

Variations on a Theme

Almost any fresh or leftover meat or vegetable can be used in the preparation of *donburi.* Possibilities include turkey, beef, veal, pork, shrimp, tuna, sardines, mushrooms, and fried bean curd. ¶ Embellish your *donburi* with artistically carved vegetable garnishes or with watercress and crumbled *nori* (dried laver).

Mail-Order Source

Dashi, mirin, sake, and *nori* are available through the mail from Katagiri & Company, 224 East 59th Street, New York, New York 10022 (212-755-3566).

✌§ Porco com Amêijoas   *Serves 4*
(POHR-coh cohm ah-MAZE-zhu-ahs)

The coastline of the province of Estremadura in western Portugal is lined with small fishing villages on whose sandy beaches rest multicolored wooden boats of striking configuration. Their crescent-shaped bows curve sharply upward — a design that helps a vessel slice through the pounding breakers as it is pushed and rowed into the Atlantic by strong-armed fishermen.

I've watched several launchings, and within hours the boats returned heavy with tuna, mackerel, and sardines. The veteran mariners guided their crafts through the churning surf and into the sandy shallows where the round-bottomed boats were hauled by rope to the safety of the upper beach. This heavy work was performed by the piscators' families and friends, or with the aid of a lumbering ox or modern tractor. Womenfolk and their children unloaded the day's catch and either sold it on the spot to wandering shoppers or carried it to the pier-side market.

Clams, too, are harvested from the coastal waters, and pigs are reared on inland farms. These two culinary mainstays of Portugal are often combined into *porco com amêijoas,* "pork with clams." You might call it the Portuguese version of America's "surf and turf."

⅔ cup dry white wine
1 teaspoon chopped garlic
½ teaspoon salt (or to taste)
1½ pounds boned pork loin
18 small hard-shell clams
2 tablespoons olive oil
½ cup chopped white onions

⅔ cup boiling water
½ cup diced tomatoes
½ teaspoon dried red pepper
   flakes
3 tablespoons chopped fresh
   coriander leaves

Steps

1. Prepare the marinade: Combine the wine, garlic, and salt in a medium-sized glass, enamel, or stainless steel bowl.
2. Cut the pork into 1-inch cubes and add them to the marinade. Turn the pork several times, cover the bowl, and store it overnight in the refrigerator, turning the meat occasionally.
3. Remove the bowl and the clams from the refrigerator 1 hour before proceeding to step 4.
4. Transfer the pork to several layers of paper towels and pat dry. Reserve the marinade.
5. Heat the olive oil in a 4- to 6-quart casserole over moderate heat. Brown the pork in batches, allowing about 3 minutes for each batch. As you brown them, transfer the pieces to a warm plate.
6. Reduce the heat to low to moderate, and sauté the onions for about 2 minutes. Stir frequently.
7. Add the pork, boiling water, marinade, tomatoes, red pepper, and 2 tablespoons of the coriander. Bring the mixture to a simmer.
8. Cover, and cook the preparation for 20 minutes over low heat.

9. Scrub the clams under hot running tap water. Discard any clam that stays open as you wash it, because that is a sign that the clam is dead and likely unwholesome.

10. Add the clams to the pot. Bring the preparation to a simmer. Cover, and cook it over low heat for 6 to 12 minutes (depending on clam size) until all the bivalves open. If any refuse to open after a reasonable cooking period, discard them; their wholesomeness is suspect.

11. Transfer the pork and clams to a large warm bowl. Arrange them attractively, and pour the sauce over them. Sprinkle the remaining coriander over your *porco com amêijoas*. Serve immediately.

Additional Keys to Success

When transferring the pork in step 4, be sure to scrape the clinging garlic particles back into the marinade bowl. Otherwise, the garlic will scorch and become bitter in the hot oil during step 5. ¶ The smaller the size of the clam for its variety, the better suited it is for this dish. On the East Coast, buy littlenecks. ¶ The Portuguese *vinho verde* is an appropriate cooking wine because of its high acid content. ¶ Do not let the cooking liquid come to a boil. Otherwise, the pork and clams will become tough. ¶ If you prematurely lift the lid in step 10, steam will escape and the clams will take longer than necessary to cook.

Serving Suggestions and Affinities

Accompany your *porco com amêijoas* with plain white rice and/or crusty bread. Serve a salad on the side. ¶ Select a fresh, young, dry white wine that has a reasonable degree of acidity.

Variations on a Theme

Shuck the clams after they are cooked in step 10. Discard the shells. ¶ Substitute parsley for the coriander leaves.

✵§ Roghan Josh   *Serves 4*
(ROH-gun JOH'SH)

Kashmir is a veritable paradise on earth. Still lingering in my memory
is one enchanted morning. I was exploring the poplar-lined canals
in a small boat, called a *shikara,* when a flotilla of shallow-bottomed
wooden vessels silently appeared out of the mist rising from the still
water. They were laden with fruits and vegetables destined for the
marketplace and, like my boat, were propelled by poles. Before they
completely passed me, I had purchased from the vendors a variety
of freshly harvested foods for my midday meal.

Later that morning my *shikara* was gliding over the mirror-smooth
surface of Dal Lake. I could see reflected in the water snowcapped
peaks of the spurs of the mighty Hindu Kush and Himalayas. Periodically my *shikara* slipped through green patches of flowering white
lotuses, all within sight of the Shalimar Gardens.

Moored against a shoreline were a string of neo-Victorian house-
boats with elaborately sculptured details — the Kashmiri wood carvers
have stellar reputations. The wall paneling inside these floating pal-
aces was even more ornately chiseled. You can rent one of these
vessels for only eighty dollars a day (about fourteen dollars per person), which includes three meals and three attentive servants: house-
boy, chef, and *shikara* chauffeur. If you're on a budget, a less opulent
houseboat runs about five dollars per day per person.

Near my houseboat a family was busily preparing a *wazwan,* a
thirty-dish feast for the peasant wedding planned that evening. *Roghan
josh,* marinated spiced lamb, was the featured specialty.

Roghan josh is simultaneously a Mogul and a peasant dish because
it has its roots in both culinary styles. The Mogul, or court, version
is prepared from a more elaborate recipe, but the peasant-style *roghan
josh* I tasted at the wedding had more vitality and character.

1½ pounds of 1¼-inch-cubed
  lean leg of lamb
½ cup whole-milk yogurt
¼ teaspoon crushed saffron
2 tablespoons water
⅓ cup coarsely chopped
  blanched almonds
Seeds of 1 cardamom pod
½ teaspoon cumin seeds
½ teaspoon coriander seeds
3 tablespoons ghee (or clarified
  butter)

⅓ cup chopped white onions
1 teaspoon minced garlic
1 tablespoon minced fresh
  ginger
3 tablespoons chopped chili
  pepper
¼ teaspoon ground turmeric
½ teaspoon salt (or to taste)
¼ cup chopped fresh coriander
  leaves

Steps

1. Marinate the lamb in the yogurt in a noncorrosible bowl overnight in the refrigerator.
2. Remove the marinating lamb from the refrigerator 1 hour before beginning step 4.
3. Preheat the oven to 400° F.
4. Soak the saffron in the water.
5. Spread the almonds and the cardamom, cumin, and coriander seeds on an oven-proof plate. Bake them in the oven for 10 minutes. (This process enhances their flavor.)
6. Heat the ghee in a large, heavy-bottomed sauté pan or skillet.
7. Sauté the onions for 2 minutes over low heat, stirring frequently. Add the garlic and ginger. Sauté the mixture for 1 minute, stirring frequently.
8. Stir in the lamb and its marinade, as well as the saffron and its soaking water. Also stir in the chili pepper, turmeric, salt, and the almonds and spices from step 5.
9. Cover the pan. Cook the preparation for 1¼ hours over low heat, stirring every 15 minutes.
10. Remove the cover and cook the preparation for 30 minutes, or until the sauce has slightly reduced and thickened. Stir frequently.
11. Add the coriander leaves. Stir the mixture for 10 seconds. Serve immediately.

Additional Keys to Success

If you — rather than the butcher — cube the lamb, cut it from the shank half. And be sure to remove fell, gristle, and surface fat from the meat. ¶ Don't substitute skim-milk yogurt for the whole-milk yogurt. ¶ If you do not have the whole spices for step 5, use the ground equivalents and roast them for only 5 minutes. ¶ If you don't have ghee or clarified butter, substitute 1½ tablespoons each of unsalted butter and vegetable oil. ¶ Don't let the preparation boil in steps 9 and 10 lest the yogurt curdle and the lamb toughen. ¶ If fresh coriander leaves are unavailable, substitute 2 tablespoons of fresh parsley leaves (preferably the flat-leaf variety).

Serving Suggestions and Affinities

Kashmirians love to eat their *roghan josh* with white rice and breads. If you can't buy Indian-style breads, you can serve pita bread. ¶ Prepare a side dish of cooked spinach or other greens. ¶ *Lassi,* a yogurt drink, is a popular beverage accompaniment. ¶ Beer is a better beverage choice than wine.

Variations on a Theme

Experiment with different spices, such as asafetida, and flavoring agents, such as tamarind. ¶ Instead of braising the lamb in step 9, cook it uncovered. Add a few tablespoons of water each time the liquid nearly evaporates. ¶ Substitute kid or beef for the lamb.

Leftovers

Roghan josh can be made a day ahead of time for a party. An overnight rest in the refrigerator produces subtle flavors.

Mail-Order Sources

Saffron, cardamom pod, cumin seeds, coriander seeds, turmeric, asafetida, and tamarind are available through the mail from Kalustyan Orient Expert Trading Corporation, 123 Lexington Avenue, New York, New York 10016 (212-685-3416). Fresh ginger is available from Katagiri & Company, 224 East 59th Street, New York, New York 10022 (212-755-3566).

✑ Ropa Vieja   *Serves 6 to 8*
(ROH-pah vee'EH hah)

My first and only trip to Cuba was in 1956, several years before Fidel
Castro took over the reins of the government. During my stay I visited
a large sugar cane plantation (now, no doubt, a government-owned
cooperative).

The season was summer and therefore the climate was hot and
rainy. It was the time to be planting sugar cane cuttings. In less than
a year the stalks would be ten feet high and nearly two inches thick.
After their harvest, the stalks would be pressed to extract their sugary
juices, which would then be reduced by evaporation into a dark, sticky
mass. Refining would transform it into white sugar.

I had dinner in the home of one of the plantation workers. His
wife cooked the Cuban specialty *ropa vieja* for me. The name for
this flavorful beef stew is Spanish and means "old clothes," because
some say the shredded meat resembles the tattered garments of a
beggar. Whatever its name, *ropa vieja* is good enough to put on a
billionaire's table.

3 pounds lean boneless beef round roast	½ cup Italian sweet peppers cut into julienne strips
1 cup cold tap water	1 cup chopped vine-ripened tomatoes
⅛ cup white wine vinegar	
1 medium-sized bay leaf	¼ cup carrots cut into julienne strips
¼ teaspoon ground cinnamon	
1 whole clove	1 teaspoon ground red pepper (cayenne)
6 annatto seeds	
¼ cup olive oil	3 tablespoons chopped coriander leaves
⅔ cup sliced white onions	
1 tablespoon minced garlic	½ teaspoon salt (or to taste)

Steps

1. Preheat the oven to 300° F.
2. Trim the exterior fat and gristle off the beef. Cut the meat into
1½-inch cubes.
3. Add the water, vinegar, bay leaf, cinnamon, clove, and annatto

seeds to a heavy-bottomed, 3- to 4-quart casserole. Bring the liquid to a simmer and stir in the beef.

4. Cover the casserole and braise the preparation in the oven for 2½ hours, turning the meat halfway through the cooking process.

5. Heat the oil in a large, heavy-bottomed sauté pan (or a 2- to 3-quart saucepan) over low to moderate heat. Sauté the onions for 2 minutes, stirring frequently. Add the garlic and sweet peppers. Sauté the mixture for 1 minute, stirring frequently.

6. Stir the tomatoes, carrots, cayenne, coriander, and salt into the onion-pepper mixture. Simmer the sauce, uncovered, over low heat for 15 minutes, stirring occasionally.

7. Transfer the meat to a warm bowl and cover it with aluminum foil. Pour the pot's cooking liquid through a sieve into the sauce. Simmer the sauce for 15 minutes, stirring occasionally.

8. Shred the beef by tearing it apart with two forks or with your fingers. Stir the beef into the sauce. Gently simmer the ingredients for 10 minutes, stirring occasionally. Transfer the meat with its sauce to a warm serving bowl. Serve promptly.

Additional Keys to Success

Top, bottom, or eye round is suitable for this dish. So is a flank steak, sirloin tip, or lean chuck roast. ¶ *Ropa vieja* can be prepared without the annatto seeds, but your dish will lack the characteristic flavor and reddish-yellow color imparted by the seeds. ¶ If the onions and garlic are sautéed over too high a heat or for too long a period in step 5, they will burn and therefore develop a sharp bitter taste. ¶ To obtain succulent beef shreds, it is essential to cook the beef for a long period with low heat. ¶ The meat will unnecessarily shrink and toughen if its cooking liquid is allowed to boil in step 3 or 4. ¶ If fresh vine-ripened tomatoes are unavailable, substitute a good brand of canned imported plum tomatoes. ¶ If you can't purchase fresh coriander leaves, substitute another herb. If you use a dried herb, keep in mind that dried herbs are generally twice as strong as fresh ones.

Serving Suggestions and Affinities

Popular side dishes for *ropa vieja* include plain rice, black beans, and fried plantains. ¶ *Ropa vieja* can be successfully paired with a medium-to full-bodied red wine that has more acidity and assertiveness than subtleties — a medium-priced Rioja usually fills the bill. Beer is another apt partner for *ropa vieja.*

Variations on a Theme

Use lard instead of olive oil. ¶ Make a thinner sauce by adding more water in step 3. For a thicker sauce, add bread crumbs in step 8. ¶ Add slivered ham in step 5. ¶ In step 6, add other vegetables — corn kernels or shredded turnips, for instance.

Leftovers

Plan for leftovers, because *ropa vieja* develops new flavor nuances as it sits for a day or two in the refrigerator.

Mail-Order Source

Annatto seeds are available through the mail from H. Roth & Son, 1577 First Avenue, New York, New York 10028 (212-734-1110).

⇜§ Sarma   *Serves 4*
   (SAHR-mah)

Stuffed pickled or fresh cabbage leaves are a dietary mainstay throughout the Balkans. In Yugoslavia, they are called *sarma,* and are eaten at least once a week by the average peasant.

My first taste of peasant-style *sarma* occurred on a radiant Sunday when I was driving through the Serbian republic in Yugoslavia. I took the wrong turn, as I am accustomed to do, and ended up on a dead-end road leading to an old farmhouse with a red-tiled roof.

My presence surprised the farmer, who was tending his beehives. Initially, he appeared resentful of my intrusion into his domain, but slowly a welcoming (or was it a forgiving?) smile crossed his face. He paused to wipe beads of sweat off his brow with a large, red handkerchief, and then motioned to me to come inside his house. Going directly to the cupboard, he pulled out a pair of drinking glasses and a bottle of slivovitz. After pouring this crystal clear plum brandy into the glasses, he handed me one and toasted our chance encounter.

My new friend led me into the kitchen to introduce me to his wife, who was just starting to make *sarma* on a wooden table next to an antique ceramic-tiled stove. Since I'd sampled *sarma* in restaurants, but never in a rural home, I volunteered to be her helper — and she accepted my offer. Two hours later I was back in my car, heading toward the proper road, with that satisfied feeling you get after eating a plateful of homemade *sarma*.

4 quarts water
1½ teaspoons salt (or to taste)
1 large head of cabbage
1 pound sauerkraut
2 tablespoons olive oil
1 cup coarsely chopped white onions
2 teaspoons chopped garlic

1 pound ground lean beef
¼ cup long-grain white rice
1 teaspoon fresh lemon juice
½ teaspoon rosemary
½ teaspoon sweet paprika
¼ cup dry white wine
½ cup tomato purée

Steps

1. Bring the water to a boil in a 6- to 8-quart pot. Stir in 1 teaspoon of the salt. Preheat the oven to 350° F.
2. Remove sixteen leaves from the cabbage head. Trim the leaves of any core portions.
3. Blanch the leaves in batches in the boiling water for 3 to 5 minutes, or until they are supple. Remove and drain the leaves.
4. Drain, rinse, and drain the sauerkraut.
5. Heat the olive oil in a large sauté pan or skillet. Sauté the onions over low to moderate heat for 2 minutes. Add the garlic and ground beef. Sauté the mixture for 3 minutes while breaking up the meat clumps.
6. Add the rice, lemon juice, rosemary, paprika, ½ cup of the sauerkraut, and the remaining salt. Vigorously mix the ingredients for about 1 minute. Turn off the heat and let stand until cool enough to handle.
7. Place approximately 2 rounded tablespoons of the meat mixture in the middle of each cabbage leaf. Wrap the leaf around the filling, envelope-style.
8. Place a ½-inch layer of sauerkraut on the bottom of a heavy casserole. Arrange the *sarma* (stuffed cabbage leaves) seam side down in

a tight-fitting layer on top of the sauerkraut. Cover the sarma with the remaining sauerkraut.

9. Mix the wine and tomato purée and pour it evenly over the sauerkraut.

10. Cover the casserole, and bake the preparation for 1 hour.

11. Serve the *sarma* hot. Accompany it with the cooked and drained sauerkraut.

Additional Keys to Success

It is essential to use a fresh, big head of cabbage in excellent condition. ¶ Be careful not to rip the leaves. Otherwise, the stuffing might ooze out during the cooking process. ¶ If you are inexperienced at peeling unbroken leaves from a cabbage, consider buying two heads. ¶ Some recipes call for cooked or partially cooked rice. Uncooked rice works best because it swells during cooking, making your stuffed-cabbage rolls plump. ¶ To ensure that the rice will steam properly, the casserole must be tightly covered in step 10.

Serving Suggestions and Affinities

Serve your *sarma* topped with yogurt, sour cream, or a thickened sauce made from the pan liquid. ¶ Rye or pumpernickel is a good bread choice. ¶ Serve beer or a hearty and fruity young red wine.

Variations on a Theme

If you can buy (or can make at home) pickled cabbage leaves, by all means use them in place of the fresh leaves. In this case, do not blanch them. Also, omit the sauerkraut from the recipe. ¶ Some cooks substitute vine or spinach leaves for the cabbage leaves. ¶ Substitute veal, pork, or lamb for the beef — or prepare a combination. ¶ For a more complex flavor, prepare the stuffing the day before and refrigerate it overnight.

Mail-Order Source

Rosemary and sweet paprika are available through the mail from Paprikás Weiss, 1546 Second Avenue, New York, New York 10028 (212-288-6117).

✑ Sauerbraten
(ZOW-ehr-BRAHT-ehn)

Serves 8 to 10

Literally, *sauerbraten* means "sour roast." It is not a dish to prepare impulsively: The beef must marinate for days in vinegar and wine infused with herbs and other aromatic flavoring agents; it is then gently cooked for several hours.

I closely associate *sauerbraten* with the Middle Rhine, the loveliest portion of the river's long journey from the snowcapped Swiss Alps to the heaving North Sea. In the Rheingau stretch, grapes grow on steep terraced vineyards along the sunny right bank and produce some of the most distinguished wines in the world. Steinberger, Schloss Johannisberger, and Schloss Vollrads are among the greats.

Castle ruins, too, cling to the precipitous slopes. Their remaining stone walls are testimony to the era when robber barons controlled the Middle Rhine, exacting burdensome tolls and thus inhibiting the free flow of commerce.

The imposing Lorelei Rock, made famous by poem and song, projects into the Rhine, creating a narrows with swift, treacherous currents. According to German legend, the enchanting singing of a seductive nymph lured mariners into being shipwrecked on the reef below her rock. I suspect that whenever she temporarily lost her voice, she tempted the sailors with a platter of steaming *sauerbraten*.

4 pounds boneless beef roast
1½ cups wine vinegar
½ cup red wine
2 cups water
2 medium-sized yellow onions, sliced
4 whole cloves
1 teaspoon caraway seeds
2 bay leaves

1 teaspoon salt (or to taste)
10 whole black peppercorns
¼ cup raisins
1 sprig parsley
2 tablespoons lard
⅓ cup chopped yellow onions
4 tablespoons chopped carrots
½ cup crushed gingersnaps

Steps

1. Trim off all exterior fat from the meat. Place the meat in a suitably deep glass, enamel, earthenware, or stainless steel bowl.
2. Prepare the marinade: Add the vinegar and the next nine ingredi-

ents to a saucepan. Bring the mixture to a boil, turn off the heat, and allow the marinade to cool. Add the parsley.

3. Pour the marinade over the meat. Turn the meat several times. Cover the bowl and store it in the warmest section of your refrigerator for four to seven days. Turn the meat twice a day.

4. Remove the bowl from the refrigerator 2 hours before beginning step 5.

5. Remove the meat from the marinade and pat it dry with paper towels. Reserve the marinade. Preheat the oven to 300° F.

6. Heat the lard in a large Dutch oven (or heavy casserole) on top of the stove. Brown the meat on all sides (this should take about 5 to 8 minutes altogether). Transfer the meat to a hot platter.

7. Sauté the onions and carrots in the fat for 2 minutes over low to medium heat, stirring frequently.

8. Return the meat to the Dutch oven. Stir the marinade and strain enough of it into the Dutch oven to come halfway up the sides of the meat. Discard any remaining marinade. Bring the preparation to a low simmer.

9. Cover the Dutch oven and place it in the oven. Braise the *sauerbraten* for 2 hours, or until tender. Turn the meat once, approximately halfway through the cooking process.

10. Transfer the cooked meat to a hot platter and loosely cover it with aluminum foil.

11. Strain approximately 2 cups of the cooking liquid into a saucepan. Bring it to a simmer. Add the gingersnaps to the liquid and simmer the sauce for 5 to 8 minutes, until it thickens slightly. Stir frequently. Adjust the seasonings to taste.

12. Carve part of the *sauerbraten* across the grain into slices at least ¼ inch thick. Arrange the slices on a hot serving platter in overlapping layers. Place the uncut *sauerbraten* piece on the platter if you wish. Spoon some of the sauce over the slices and serve the remaining sauce in a hot bowl. Garnish the platter with sprigs of fresh herbs and, if you prepare them, such accompaniments as dumplings and vegetables. Serve immediately.

Additional Keys to Success

Rump is the best cut of beef for *sauerbraten*. Bottom, top, or eye round is also suitable. Chuck is satisfactory if lean. ¶ It is not necessary to have exactly 4 pounds of beef for this recipe as long as you stay in the 3½-to-4½-pound range. ¶ Some recipes call for larding. This bothersome procedure is necessary only when you are cooking a roast from an old and sinewy animal (unlikely in America) or if you are pan-roasting the meat without a lid. If you prefer the extra flavor that the fat lends to the dish, add extra fat to the braising liquid and skim the excess fat just prior to making the sauce. ¶ If the roast is not compact, tie it with a string. Remove the string just before slicing. ¶ Warning: Though an earthenware bowl is the traditional marinating vessel, do not use one unless you are positive that its glaze has been fired by the potter at a very high temperature. Otherwise, you run the risk of lead poisoning (the high acidity of the marinade may leach out the lead contained in the glaze). ¶ Some American recipes call for sugar. Most German peasant cooks prefer to use the sweetening power of dried fruit, such as raisins. ¶ If you have a consistently cool spot in your home (approximately 50° F), you need not refrigerate the marinating beef as long as the meat remains entirely submerged. ¶ The longer you marinate the beef, the more sour a flavor it will develop. I've marinated *sauerbraten* for ten days with superb results. What I don't recommend is marinating the meat for less than four days, as some American cooks advise. If you do, the meat will not be sufficiently tart to be a legitimate *sauerbraten*. ¶ If you don't have the lard for step 6, substitute 1 tablespoon each of vegetable oil and unsalted butter. ¶ Some recipes call for stove-top braising. This method produces results inferior to the oven braising method. ¶ Some recipes specify a higher braising temperature and a correspondingly shorter cooking period. My "300° F for 2 hours" formula helps ensure maximum flavor, juiciness, and tenderness — as well as minimum shrinkage. At no time should the mixture boil in steps 8 and 9. ¶ If you don't have gingersnaps, thicken the sauce with a slurry comprising 4 tablespoons each of flour and cold water. Thoroughly mix the flour and water in a small bowl and then, while stirring continuously, slowly add it to the sauce. To compensate for the sweetness that would have been provided by the gingersnaps, add ⅛ cup of chopped dried fruit of your choice. Simmer the sauce for 5 to 8 minutes and stir it frequently. ¶ If the meat is carved too thin, the slices may fall apart. ¶ Germans love to sauce the *sauerbraten* slices generously.

Variations on a Theme

Add six juniper berries to the marinade. ¶ Rather than braising the meat, pan-roast it in a rack set in a pan containing some of the marinade (replenish the liquid as it evaporates). This method requires larding and/or frequent basting. ¶ Add to the braising liquid ingredients such as beef marrow, tomato purée, mustard, thyme, and allspice. ¶ Approximately 30 minutes before the meat is done, add some new potatoes and/or whole baby carrots to the pot. ¶ Thicken the sauce with heavy cream rather than with gingersnaps.

Serving Suggestions and Affinities

Popular starch accompaniments include bread or potato dumplings; spaetzle; potato pancakes; noodles tossed in butter; hot potato salad; baked, mashed, braised, or pan-roasted new potatoes; crusty bread. ¶ Also consider serving red cabbage, applesauce, stewed dried fruit, carrots and/or a green vegetable or green salad. ¶ Best beverage bets are beer; Gewürztraminer wine; dry to semidry, medium- to full-bodied Rhine or Mosel wine; robust, dry, medium- to full-bodied red wine.

Mail-Order Source

Whole cloves, caraway seeds, whole black peppercorns, and juniper berries are available through the mail from H. Roth & Son, 1577 First Avenue, New York, New York 10028 (212-734-1110).

◆§ Schweinehaxen

Serves 4

(SHVIGH-nuh-HAHX-uhn)

Bavaria is Germany's most scenic state. On its southern edge rise the solemn Bavarian Alps. When skiing there, I often paused to listen to the ethereal whispers of the frigid winds swirling around the icy mountain passes and peaks high above.

The Alps gradually give way to rolling lands of dense forest inhabited by deer, wild boar, and cunning hunters. What is not forest is mainly devoted to rearing livestock and raising wheat, hops, and other cash crops. Green is the predominant color of Bavaria, except in winter, when the land becomes pristine white.

The hub of each farm is usually a two- or three-story building with living quarters at one end and the barn at the other. Heavy midwinter snowdrifts in the region make this architectural plan essential for reaching the sheltered animals.

Bavarian farmhouses such as these are frequently quite old, many having been passed down from generation to generation. Most are designed with a long wooden balcony sporting potted flowers, and with a low-pitched roof weighted down by stones. Quaint names and scenes are often painted on the outside white walls.

I learned how to prepare *schweinehaxen* in one of these friendly homes. Though the primary ingredient of this dish was only pork knuckles, the Hausman family paid me more honor when they served it to me than I could possibly deserve.

2 tablespoons lard (or butter)
4 1¼-pound pork knuckles
½ cup chopped white onions
4 tablespoons chopped carrots
½ cup vinegar
1 teaspoon honey

½ teaspoon prepared mustard
1 bay leaf
Heaping ½ teaspoon salt (or to taste)
¼ teaspoon freshly ground black pepper

Steps

1. Preheat the oven to 275° F.
2. Melt the lard in a 5- to 6-quart wide-bottomed casserole on top of the stove over moderate heat. Add two of the pork knuckles and

brown all the exposed meat. Transfer these knuckles to a warm platter and loosely cover them with foil. Brown the two remaining knuckles and transfer them to the platter, too.

3. Sauté the onions for 1 minute in the casserole over low heat. Add the carrots and sauté the mixture for 3 additional minutes.

4. Stir in the vinegar, honey, mustard, bay leaf, salt, and pepper. Bring the mixture to a simmer.

5. Return the knuckles to the casserole. Coat them with the mixture by turning them in the pot.

6. Bake the casserole in the middle of the oven for 2½ hours, turning the knuckles over halfway through the cooking period.

7. Transfer the knuckles to a warm platter and serve immediately. If you wish, serve the sauce in a bowl on the side.

Additional Keys to Success

Small pork knuckles (sometimes called pork shanks) are necessary because each diner should be served his own *schweinehaxen* on the bone. ¶ Do not trim off the excess fat — it is an essential part of the dish. ¶ The meat will unnecessarily shrink and toughen if you bake the *schweinehaxen* at a temperature much higher than 275° F. ¶ A 2½-hour cooking period is necessary because when the *schweinehaxen* are done the meat should shred and fall off the bone with nothing more than the aid of a fork.

Serving Suggestions and Affinities

Sauerkraut is a popular partner. So are potatoes, especially if they are steamed, baked, mashed, or prepared as pancakes. Another traditional starch is rye or pumpernickel bread. ¶ A hearty beer is the best beverage accompaniment.

Variations on a Theme

Pickle the knuckles for one to seven days in a seasoned vinegar-water marinade; then braise them in ½ cup of the marinade. ¶ Gently simmer the knuckles in a vinegar-spiked stock for 2½ hours; then drain the knuckles and roast them for 20 minutes in a preheated 400° F oven.

◄ Somen
(soh-men)

Serves 3 to 4

The traditional Japanese dwelling may be judged flimsy by Western standards, but its flexible, modular design can better survive the devastating effects of an earthquake than would a typical house in California. "My countrymen experience many earthquakes," exclaimed my Japanese host at his farmhouse outside Tokyo. "Should a severe one occur, it is better to have a shoji screen fall on your head than a ton of bricks."

Japanese homes are practical in yet another way. Japan is overpopulated, and thus living space is at a premium. Consequently, the Japanese must build small houses and maximize the use of space. The main (and perhaps only large) room in a house can be used for a number of functions: sitting, eating, and sleeping. To convert it from a dining room to a bedroom, for instance, you simply remove the small portable dining table and lay the thin mattress, called a *futon,* on the straw-mat *tatami* floor. Moreover, the large room can be subdivided with sliding panels. Adaptability is the key.

"We Japanese are also practical when it comes to eating in the middle of summer," my host continued. "To make my point, I'm going to serve you some thin wheat noodles that my wife cooked and chilled earlier today." It took only a few bites for me to understand the wisdom of the Japanese preference for cool foods on hot and muggy days. The next time a heat wave hits your area, consider preparing a bowl of cool and refreshing *somen* for lunch.

1 pound *somen* (thin wheat
  noodles)
¼ cup soy sauce
¼ cup rice vinegar

1 tablespoon minced fresh
  ginger
3 tablespoons chopped scallions
1 small cucumber

Steps

1. Boil the noodles according to the package directions.
2. Drain the noodles and transfer them to a mixing bowl. While the noodles are still hot, gently but thoroughly toss them with the remaining ingredients except the cucumber.

3. Cover the bowl, and refrigerate the preparation for at least 3 hours.
4. Transfer the noodles to a chilled glass serving bowl or to individual bowls. Slice the cucumber. Garnish the noodles with the slices. Serve immediately.

Additional Keys to Success

If *somen* are unavailable, use thin Italian noodles, such as capellini. ¶ Do not overcook the noodles or they will become mushy.

Serving Suggestions and Affinities

Somen is eaten with chopsticks. ¶ Accompany *somen* with sake, beer, or iced tea.

Variations on a Theme

Add *mirin* (sweet *sake*) and chopped reconstituted dried Japanese mushrooms to your preparation. Or add cooked whole baby shrimp. ¶ Garnish the cold *somen* with chopped chives or crumbled *nori* (dried laver). ¶ Rather than tossing the other ingredients into the *somen* in step 2, dilute the mixture with *dashi* or water and serve it on the side as a dipping sauce for the plain noodles. ¶ Make a Japanese cold noodle dish with *soba* (buckwheat noodles).

Mail-Order Source

Somen, rice vinegar, fresh ginger, *mirin,* Japanese dried mushrooms, *nori, dashi,* and *soba* are available through the mail from Katagiri & Company, 224 East 59th Street, New York, New York 10022 (212-755-3566).

ᥤᵍ Toad-in-the-Hole   *Serves 4*

Toad-in-the-hole — sausages or other meat baked in a batter — is consumed throughout rural and urban England. Yorkshire cooks seem to prepare the best versions, perhaps because they are so adept at making Yorkshire pudding. These culinary specialties call for similar batters.

I learned how to make a proper toad-in-the-hole in a gritstone cottage situated in one of the many valleys of the Yorkshire Dales. As you drive through this historically rich region, your eye catches the ruins of abbeys, priories, and castles, each with a tale to tell. Students of history, for instance, will recall that Bolton Castle is where Mary Queen of Scots spent one of her many imprisonments.

Yorkshire Dales — now a national park — is an unofficial monument to peace and solitude. Some of the land is in its original wild state, though other areas are daubed with fenced pastureland holding sheep and cattle. Stone bridges built centuries ago cross gushing cold-water streams originating in the Pennine Chain, "the backbone of England," which stretches from Scotland to the heart of the nation.

Providing a striking contrast to the farm and grazing land in the grassy valleys are the moorland heights in the Pennines. The lonely, rocky, heather-infused terrain is aptly depicted in Emily Brontë's classic novel *Wuthering Heights*.

1 cup flour	3 tablespoons melted unsalted
½ teaspoon salt (or to taste)	butter
1 cup milk	¾ pound fresh small sausages
2 large eggs	1 tablespoon unsalted butter

Steps

1. Combine the flour and salt in a mixing bowl. Make a well in the center of the dry ingredients. Gradually pour the milk into the well while beating the mixture with a whisk or electric beater.
2. Beat the eggs lightly. Add them and the melted butter to the batter and beat it until smooth and frothy.
3. Cover the bowl, and store the batter in a cool area of your kitchen for 1 hour.
4. Preheat the oven to 425° F.
5. Pierce each sausage in several places. Place the sausages in a large sauté pan or skillet containing a ⅛-inch layer of cold water. Bring the water to a simmer, turning the sausages once. Cover the pan and simmer for 5 minutes. Remove the lid and continue to cook until the water evaporates and the links become lightly brown in their rendered fat. Turn the sausages often.
6. Grease a 2-inch-deep, 2-quart rectangular baking pan (about 7

inches wide by 11 inches long) with the tablespoon of unsalted butter.

7. Slice the sausages into 1-inch-long segments.

8. Arrange the sausages in neat rows in the baking dish. Each segment should be separated as much as possible from the others and from the walls of the dish.

9. Pour the batter over the sausages. Reposition the pattern if you disturb it.

10. Place the pan on the middle rack of the oven and bake for 25 to 30 minutes, or until the batter puffs up and turns golden brown.

11. Remove from oven, cut into individual portions, and serve immediately.

Additional Keys to Success

If you use the standard supermarket variety of sausages, you'll probably have to pour off some of the excess water after you remove the lid in step 5. Reason: These mass-produced sausages typically have a relatively high water content. ¶ Unless the oven is preheated to about 425° F, the batter won't puff up sufficiently. If the temperature is much higher than 425° F, the surface of the batter will burn before the rest of the batter is fully baked. ¶ A delay in serving will cause your toad-in-the-hole to deflate.

Variations on a Theme

Substitute small pieces of steak, ham, or kidneys for the sausages. ¶ Some cooks construct the dish in three layers: batter, sausages, batter. Other cooks place the sausages on top of the batter. ¶ Spread ½ cup beef drippings on the bottom and sides of the pan. Heat the pan in the oven for 5 minutes. Then add the sausages and batter. If you follow this variation, eliminate the butter from the recipe.

Serving Suggestions

Prepare toad-in-the-hole for your next brunch. It's a big hit among children of all ages.

❧ Vatapá

(vah-tah-PAH)

Serves 4

Soon after the Portuguese navigator Cabral claimed Brazil in 1500, slaves from Africa were being imported in great numbers to Bahia, in northeastern Brazil, to work the sugar cane plantations. Over the years a racial mixture called mulatto began to emerge, and eventually it became the dominant population group. The mulattos of Brazil are people of three continents — the blood of black slaves, white settlers, and native Indians runs in their veins.

More than blood blended. An amalgamated cuisine developed, borrowing from the culinary styles and ingredients of West Africa, Europe, and South America. A dish that is typical of this melting-pot cuisine is the Bahian specialty called *vatapá,* a hot and spicy stew cooked with *dendê* (palm nut) oil and coconut milk. The main ingredient can be seafood or meat.

I enjoyed a *vatapá* made of dried shrimp and fresh fish in a fisherman's palm-sheltered hut along Bahia's beautiful coastline. Like most Bahians, my host and his family were quick to smile and went out of their way to make strangers feel at ease and welcomed. But the grandmother of the house made the most delightful impression on me — she prepared the *vatapá* that would please almost any guest, as this recipe will verify.

¼ pound dried shrimp
1½ pounds halibut or other firm-fleshed, nonoily fish
2 cups coconut milk
2 tablespoons *dendê* (palm nut) oil
½ cup chopped onions
1 tablespoon minced garlic
2 cups water
1 bay leaf
¼ cup chopped fresh chili peppers
1 teaspoon salt (or to taste)
⅓ cup freshly ground unsalted, shelled, skinned, and roasted peanuts
¼ cup fine-grained cornmeal

Steps

1. Chop the shrimp in a food processor or electric blender.
2. Bone and skin the fish. Discard the skin. Reserve the bones for step 3. Cut the fish into 1-inch cubes and reserve them for step 8.

3. Add the shrimp, coconut milk, and fish bones to a thick-bottomed 1½- to 2-quart saucepan. Bring the mixture to a simmer, stirring occasionally. Simmer the mixture for 30 minutes, stirring now and then.

4. Heat the oil in a thick-bottomed 2- to 3-quart saucepan over low to moderate heat. Sauté the onions for 2 minutes, stirring frequently. Add the garlic and sauté this mixture for 1 minute, stirring constantly.

5. Stir 1¾ cups of the water into the onion-garlic mixture. Stir in the bay leaf, chili peppers, salt, and peanuts. Bring the mixture to a simmer and cook it for 10 minutes.

6. Discard the bay leaf from the onion-garlic preparation. Strain into this preparation the shrimp-coconut mixture. Simmer the combination for 5 minutes.

7. Soak the cornmeal in the remaining ¼ cup water for 5 minutes. Slowly stir the moist cornmeal into the pot. Simmer the mixture for 5 minutes, stirring occasionally.

8. Add the fish cubes to the pot. Thoroughly submerge them and gently cook the preparation over low heat for 5 to 7 minutes, stirring occasionally and very gently. Serve the *vatapá* immediately.

Additional Keys to Success

If palm nut oil is unavailable, use olive oil. Also substitute ½ cup puréed tomatoes for the ¼ cup of the water in step 7; this gives the dish some of its characteristic reddish hue that would otherwise have been imparted by the palm nut oil. ¶ When handling the chili peppers, do not touch your eyes. Thoroughly wash the knife blade, your hands, and the work surface when you complete the cutting task. ¶ Adjust the quantity of chili according to your degree of built-up immunity to that spice — but, remember, *vatapá* is supposed to be hot. ¶ Substitutes for halibut include cod and striped sea bass. ¶ Do not let the coconut milk boil for even a second throughout the recipe.

Serving Suggestions and Affinities

Ladle your *vatapá* into shallow soup bowls — by the time the preparation is cooked, it will have the consistency of a thin porridge. ¶ One of the traditional accompaniments to *vatapá* is *pirao de arroz com leite de coco,* a cold pudding made with rice flour and coconut milk. Plain rice — served steaming hot — is also popular. ❡ Cold beer is the preferred alcoholic beverage for *vatapá.*

Variations on a Theme

Add some shelled and deveined fresh shrimp to the recipe 1 or 2 minutes after you add the fish in step 8. ❡ Use tomatoes whether or not you use palm nut oil. ❡ Substitute almonds or cashew nuts for the peanuts. Brazil nuts can be used, too. ❡ Experiment by adding ginger and other flavoring agents. Diced sweet green peppers lend color contrast. ❡ In place of the cornmeal, use manioc, rice flour, cornstarch, or bread crumbs to thicken the dish. ❡ Use pork or chicken as the main ingredient.

Mail-Order Source

Coconut milk, *dendê* (palm nut) oil, fine-grained cornmeal, ginger, manioc, and rice flour are available through the mail from Casa Moneo Spanish Imports, 210 West 14th Street, New York, New York 10011 (212-929-1644).

⋖⸹ Yassa   *Serves 4*
(yah-sᴀʜ)

West African women are known for their patterned, color-rich apparel, but nowhere is their clothing as graphically bold as in Senegal. This love of fashion is not restricted to the cosmopolitan capital, Dakar. I've seen Senegalese women from various hinterland villages walking in stately elegance with their distinct, multicolored, flowing gowns and wrapped headgear — they would not be out of place sauntering down Fifth Avenue.

In one of these villages I was introduced to *yassa,* the spicy chicken dish beloved throughout this region of Africa. Two hours before cooking time, the cook marinated the meat, partly to infuse it with extra flavor and partly to help preserve it. The latter measure is often necessary for meat dishes in the tropics because few rural cooks have any means of refrigeration to protect the food from the pathogenic bacteria fostered by the torrid midday sun.

Like many Senegalese dishes, *yassa* has a pronounced lemony note and offers an exciting blend of flavors. I doubt that *yassa* could bore even the most jaded palate.

4 small chicken legs
½ cup freshly squeezed lemon
   juice
¼ cup thinly sliced chili peppers
1 bay leaf
½ teaspoon salt (or to taste)

4 tablespoons peanut (or other
   vegetable) oil
⅔ cup sliced scallions
1 tablespoon chopped fresh
   parsley

Steps

1. Marinate the chicken legs for 2 hours at room temperature in the lemon juice, chili, bay leaf, and salt. Turn the legs occasionally.
2. Transfer the chicken to paper towels and pat dry. Reserve the marinade for step 4.
3. Heat the oil in a thick, wide-bottomed sauté pan over moderate heat. Brown the chicken on all sides.
4. Pour off all but 1 tablespoon of the oil. Stir in the scallions. Thirty seconds later, stir in the marinade. Bring the preparation to a simmer. Cover the pan and simmer for 25 to 35 minutes (depending on the thickness of the pieces). Turn the chicken once, halfway through the cooking period.
5. Transfer the chicken to a warm serving platter. Spoon the scallions, chilies, and some of the sauce over the chicken. Sprinkle the parsley over the preparation and serve immediately.

Additional Keys to Success

For the sake of color contrast, buy red chili peppers. ❡ When handling the peppers, never touch your eyes. After preparing the peppers, promptly wash the knife blade, your hands, and the cutting surface. ❡ If you can't buy fresh chili peppers, substitute 1 teaspoon of ground cayenne pepper. Do not incorporate it into the recipe until step 4. Otherwise, the pepper will burn and become bitter as the chicken browns. ❡ Adjust the quantity of chili in keeping with your tolerance for that seasoning.

Serving Suggestions and Affinities

Serve yams, sweet potatoes, or steamed rice on the side along with okra or spinach. ¶ Beer is the best alcoholic beverage accompaniment. Forget about wine — the hot and lemony *yassa* will overpower it.

Variations on a Theme

Yassa can also be made with almost any other kind of animal, bird, or crustacean meat. Fish can be used, too, if it is firm-fleshed. ¶ Substitute palm nut oil for the peanut oil.

Mail-Order Source

Palm nut oil is available through the mail from Casa Moneo Spanish Imports, 210 West 14th Street, New York, New York 10011 (212-929-1644).

Side Dishes ❧

৺ Bamia   *Serves 4*

(**B A H M**-y'ah)

My hotel room in Luxor, Egypt, overlooked the Nile. From my window I could see feluccas, the traditional river boats of the Nile, with their unique sails ablaze in the golden rays of the rising sun. Having once owned a sailboat, I wanted to experience what it would be like to captain a twenty-five-foot boat dwarfed by a fifty-foot-high sail.

I sauntered down to the river embankment to make inquiries about renting a felucca. The owner of one of the boats said he would rent me his vessel, providing that he came along as crew, just in case something went awry. It was a deal, and off I sailed down the Nile, holding a tiller as crude and bulky as a two-by-four.

Hidden behind the limestone cliffs on the left bank was the Valley of the Kings, the burial grounds for the boy-king Tutankhamen and at least sixty-three other Pharaohs. On my right passed the colossal temples of Luxor and Karnak, supported by soaring columns with lotus-motif capitals.

It was now time to return to Luxor. I came about, turning the felucca upriver. Only then did I fully comprehend the practicality of the oversized sail. I had to fight the steady current of the Nile with only a moderate breeze to help me. Without the massive sail to catch this wind, the boat would have gradually drifted several hundred miles downstream to Cairo, a prospect that neither I nor the boat's owner cherished.

Greeting our return to Luxor was the sailor's bright-eyed seven-year-old daughter with urgent news that his family was patiently waiting for him to share their midday meal (the fault for the delay was mine, since it took me more than two hours to sail but two miles upstream). I was asked if I wanted to join them, and I quickly said

155

naam — "yes" in Arabic. The memorable dish at this meal was *bamia,* the savory okra stew of the Land of the Pharaohs.

1½ tablespoons olive oil
⅔ cup sliced white onions
2 teaspoons minced garlic
1½ cups chopped tomatoes
1 tablespoon fresh lemon juice
2 tablespoons chopped fresh parsley
2 teaspoons ground coriander seed

½ teaspoon ground cardamom seed
¼ teaspoon freshly ground black pepper
Scant ½ teaspoon salt (or to taste)
1½ pounds fresh small okra

Steps

1. Heat the oil in a medium-sized, thick-bottomed sauté pan or skillet over low to moderate heat.
2. Sauté the onions for 2 minutes, stirring frequently.
3. Add the garlic and sauté the mixture for 1 minute, stirring frequently.
4. Stir in all the remaining ingredients except the okra. Bring the mixture to a simmer and cook it for 5 minutes, stirring occasionally.
5. Cut off and discard the tips and caps of each okra. Slice the okra into ½-inch segments.
6. Stir in the okra, and bring the preparation to a simmer. Cook it for 6 to 10 minutes (young okra will take the least time). Stir occasionally. Serve immediately.

Additional Keys to Success

All other variables being equal, the smaller the okra, the better the vegetable. ¶ Don't use frozen okra — the texture is too mushy. ¶ Be careful not to burn the onions or garlic in steps 2 and 3 by cooking them for too long or using too high a heat. ¶ If fresh, vine-ripened tomatoes are unavailable, use a good brand of imported Italian plum tomatoes. ¶ Don't cover the pan or overcook the preparation in step 6. Otherwise, the okra pieces will lose their vivid green hue.

Serving Suggestions and Affinities

Bamia is a commendable vegetable side dish for roast leg of lamb, or for any other roasted meat. ❡ Serve *bamia* along with plain rice — the two side dishes complement each other well.

Variations on a Theme
Cook the okra whole (after cutting off the tips and caps). Allow a few extra minutes' cooking time. ❡ Add ground or chopped lamb (or any other meat) to the recipe.

Mail-Order Source
Coriander seeds and cardamom seeds are available through the mail from H. Roth & Son, 1577 First Avenue, New York, New York 10028 (212-734-1110).

☙ Brunede Kartofler　　　　　　　*Serves 4*
(BROO-neh-deh kahr-TOHF-lehr)

Denmark is blessed with small, meticulously tended farmsteads. Dairy cattle, of course, are a common sight because they yield the rich milk that makes the words *butter* and *Denmark* almost synonymous.

Forests, lakes, white sandy beaches, and tidy fishing and agricultural villages also beautify Denmark — to the delight of urban Danes and foreign tourists alike. Despite a recent surge in industrialization and urban sprawl, the countryside still reigns supreme in this nation.

Rural Danes are a healthy and robust lot with surplus energy and gusto. Perhaps they owe their gift to the clean, crisp air that blows off the North Sea.

These folks are among the most hospitable people in the world. They are eager to make friends with strangers, and on the strength of your smile, they will invite you into their dwelling to share the family meal. On a cold winter night in one of these accommodating homes, I was served caramelized potatoes of such perfection that I made sure to learn the secret before saying my farewell. Here is the recipe for *brunede kartofler.*

2 quarts water	4 tablespoons sugar
2 teaspoons salt (or to taste)	3 tablespoons unsalted butter
2 pounds small new potatoes	1 tablespoon chopped fresh dill

Steps

1. Bring the water and salt to a rapid boil in a 4- to 5-quart pot.
2. Add the unpeeled potatoes. Bring the liquid to a simmer. Continue to simmer the potatoes for 20 minutes, or until the centers of the potatoes can be easily pierced with the point of a sharp knife.
3. Drain the potatoes. Peel them as soon as they are cool enough to handle.
4. Melt and lightly brown the sugar in a large, heavy-bottomed skillet over low heat. Stir constantly.
5. Add the butter and stir steadily until it is thoroughly blended into the caramelized sugar.
6. Add the first batch of potatoes (do not crowd the pan). Completely coat them with the caramelized mixture by shaking the pan and, if necessary, by gently rolling the potatoes with a wooden spoon.
7. Remove the glazed potatoes and keep them warm while you glaze the next batch(es).
8. Sprinkle your *brunede kartofler* with the dill and serve immediately.

Additional Keys to Success

Use firm potatoes. ¶ Do not cook at too high a heat or the sugar and butter will scorch, producing a bitter off-flavor. ¶ Do not overcook the potatoes lest they crumble. ¶ If fresh dill is unavailable, substitute fresh parsley.

Serving Suggestions and Affinities

Brunede kartofler makes a tempting side dish for pork roasts. It also complements braised or sautéed pork chops, roast beef or poultry, and baked ham.

◄§ Ensalada de Aguacate y Tomate   *Serves 2 to 4*
(en-sah-LAH-dah deh ah-gwah-KAH-teh ee toh-MAH-teh)

Guatemala is a festival of colors. In the Highlands (Los Altos), the natives are walking rainbows, especially on market days, when the peasants don their traditional striped and patterned garments, hand-woven from vivid red, yellow, blue, and green yarns.

I particularly enjoyed visiting the marketplaces of most of the dozen villages — each named after one of the Twelve Apostles — that are sprinkled around the mile-high Lake Atitlán. This body of deep-blue water is majestically framed by verdant mountains and volcanoes reaching yet another mile into the sky.

Set before the vendors in the open-air markets were foods of the region, including avocados, tomatoes, onions, lemons, chilies, and eggs — all principal ingredients of the colorful specialty *ensalada de aguacate y tomate* (literally, "avocado and tomato salad") that I learned to make during my stay. Its hues should brighten any table and its taste and texture should enliven any palate.

2 ripe avocados
2 hard-cooked large eggs
3 medium-sized vine-ripened
tomatoes
¼ cup diced yellow onions

2 tablespoons minced fresh chili
pepper
3 tablespoons fresh lemon juice
½ teaspoon salt (or to taste)
Lettuce leaves

Steps

1. Peel and remove the seeds from the avocados. Shell the eggs. Cut the avocados, eggs, and tomatoes into ⅓-inch cubes. Place these ingredients, along with the onions and chili, into a noncorrosible mixing bowl.
2. Mix the lemon juice and salt. Pour this dressing over the avocado-egg-tomato-onion-chili mixture. Thoroughly but gently toss the ingredients.
3. Refrigerate the salad for at least 1 hour.
4. Mound the salad on lettuce leaves in a bowl or on a plate. Serve immediately.

Additional Keys to Success

To ripen an avocado at home, store the fruit at room temperature in a generously pierced paper bag for 12 to 36 hours, depending on the original degree of ripeness. The avocado is ripe when it yields to gentle finger pressure as you cradle it in your hands. If the fruit was rock-hard when you purchased it, the avocado was picked prematurely and therefore will rot before it properly ripens. ¶ When mincing the chilies, do not touch your eyes. Wash the knife blade, your hands, and the work surface when you complete the task. ¶ Adjust the quantity of chili according to your built-up immunity to that spice. However, the salad should display some hotness if it is to be authentic. ¶ Do not dally between steps 1 and 2, and be sure to thoroughly toss the ingredients with the dressing. Otherwise, the uncoated avocado surfaces might brown, despite the acid content of the tomatoes.

Serving Suggestions and Affinities

This salad is splendid fare for a light lunch, especially on a hot summer day. ¶ For beauty's sake, select a serving bowl or plate made of glazed pottery, clear glass, or white ceramic. ¶ Serve tortillas or deep-fried tortilla chips on the side. ¶ Because of the lemon juice, table wines do not marry well with this salad. Sangria or beer does.

Variations on a Theme

Add one or more of these ingredients to your salad: diced pineapple, crumbled bacon, diced ham, chopped fresh parsley or coriander leaves, and garlic croutons. ¶ Substitute lime juice or vinegar for the lemon juice. When using vinegar, use only 1½ tablespoons.

⋖ᔔ Gnocchi di Patate   *Serves 4 to 6*
(NYOHK-kee dee pah-TAH-teh)

Nestled in the Alban Hills overlooking Rome stands Frascati, a quiet town noted for its beguiling gardens and Renaissance villas, many built by the Roman nobility. Even today, well-to-do Romans use Frascati as a weekend escape from the hectic pace of big-city life.

Frascati is even more renowned for its white wine. It is so widely available throughout Europe and the United States that the wine has placed the town on the gastronomic map. Frascati is by no means one of Italy's great wines. Nevertheless, the better Frascati specimens have a distinctive charm, a characteristic straw-colored hue, and a modest price tag.

Frascati comes in three styles — dry, semidry, and sweet. I prefer the dry version, as did the farmer who poured me a glass while I watched his wife prepare one of his family's favorite dishes: *gnocchi di patate,* poached potato and flour dumplings crowned with melted butter and Parmesan cheese. The handsome, dark-haired woman had deftly kneaded the cream-colored *gnocchi* dough with her powerful yet delicate hands. While transferring the dumplings to a pot of steaming water, she accidentally dropped a few on the floor, but she overcame her embarrassment with a hearty laugh.

When I prepare *gnocchi di patate* with her recipe, I sometimes open a bottle of dry Frascati for memory's sake. Or, I pour a light-to-medium-bodied red wine, such as one of the better-quality Valpolicellas, because of their affinity with the Parmesan cheese.

2 pounds boiling potatoes
Salt
Olive oil
1¼ to 1¾ cups flour
Yolks of 2 large eggs, beaten

¼ cup melted unsalted butter
¼ cup freshly grated Parmesan
 cheese
Freshly ground black pepper

Steps

1. Preheat the oven to 200° F.
2. Add at least 4 inches of water to a wide, heavy-bottomed pan. For each quart of water, add ½ teaspoon of salt (or to taste) and ½ teaspoon of olive oil. Bring the liquid to a rapid boil.
3. Boil the unpeeled potatoes for 30 to 50 minutes, depending on their thickness.
4. With a slotted spoon, transfer the potatoes to a colander. (Keep the water boiling for step 8.) Peel the potatoes as soon as they are cool enough to handle.
5. Mash the potatoes in a large bowl. Using a potato masher or wooden spoon, or your hands, gradually blend in 1¼ cups of the flour. Blend in the egg yolks.
6. Knead the dough gently for 1 to 2 minutes in the bowl with floured hands. Add up to ½ cup extra flour as you knead the dough if it has not become smooth and cohesive. (The amount of flour you need to add will depend principally on the variety of the potatoes and flour and the length of time these two ingredients have been stored.)
7. With floured hands, roll the dough into *gnocchi:* cylinders measuring approximately ½ inch in diameter and 1 inch in length. Keep the *gnocchi* separated so they don't stick together.

8. With a slotted spoon, carefully add the *gnocchi* to the rapidly boiling water. Since crowding the pan will cause some of the *gnocchi* to stick together, you'll have to cook them in batches. As each one floats to the surface (a sign that it is cooked), transfer it to a clean kitchen towel on top of a baking sheet placed in the middle of the oven. Keep the *gnocchi* separated.

9. Transfer the *gnocchi* to a warm serving bowl as soon as all of them have been cooked. Add the melted butter and sprinkle the cheese over the *gnocchi*. Give your dish a few twists of the pepper mill and toss lightly. Serve immediately.

Additional Keys to Success

The potatoes will be hard to peel if they are allowed to cool. ¶ Remember, you are making light and airy peasant-style *gnocchi* rather than restaurant- or factory-style *gnocchi*, which tend to be a bit heavy and gummy. Therefore, be prepared to leave some small lumps of potatoes and some flecks of flour and yolk in your *gnocchi* dough. If you attempt to rid your dough entirely of these "defects," you will be overmashing and overkneading the dough, and your *gnocchi* will have an unappetizing, gummy consistency. For much the same reasons, do not try to shape the *gnocchi* in step 7 into near-perfect cylinders.

Serving Suggestions

Gnocchi di patate can be served as the pasta course or as a side dish.

Variations on a Theme

Transform your *gnocchi* into ridged crescents. Using your thumb, press each segment against the concave surface of the tines of a table fork. ¶ Briefly run the *gnocchi di patate* under the broiler before serving the dish. ¶ Because of the relatively neutral dough, *gnocchi* lend themselves to a wide variety of sauces besides the one specified in this recipe. Almost any type of sauce that could be used for pasta makes happy music with *gnocchi*.

✌ Houskové Knedlíky   *Serves 4*
(HOH-skoh-vay K'NED-lee-kee)

Czechoslovakia, as its name might suggest, is at least two countries in one. The Czechs live in the western part of this landlocked nation, the Slovaks at the other end. (In between lies yet another province, Moravia.)

I've noticed a difference between the Czech and Slovak cuisines. The latter is influenced by neighboring Hungary. Slovaks, for instance, prefer wine over beer.

Czechs are beer drinkers, and they make some of the best beer in the world. Genuine Pilsner beer, made in its hometown of Plzeň, has enviable character, a quality lacking in most American beers. The Czechs acquired their love of beer and hearty fare from their westerly neighbors, the Germans and Austrians.

Czechs adore dumplings. The national favorite is a rich bread dumpling called *houskové knedlíky*. During a drive through the Bohemian countryside in search of the quintessential *houskové knedlíky*, my Czech companion told me her theory: "These dumplings are largely responsible for the excess weight my countrymen tote around." An occasional serving of *houskové knedlíky* shouldn't cause undue alarm. I never gained a pound during my stay in Czechoslovakia, and I greedily devoured more than my fair share of these savory dumplings.

3 quarts water
2 teaspoons salt (or to taste)
6 slices slightly stale white bread
4 tablespoons unsalted butter
1 cup flour
½ teaspoon baking powder
Yolks of 2 large eggs, beaten

2 tablespoons chopped scallions
1 tablespoon chopped fresh
   parsley
⅛ teaspoon freshly ground black
   pepper
⅝ cup whole milk

Steps

1. Bring the water and 1½ teaspoons of the salt to a rapid boil in a wide-bottomed 4½- to 6-quart pot.
2. Trim off the crust and cut the bread into ½-inch cubes.
3. Melt the butter in a large sauté pan or skillet. Sauté the bread

cubes for several minutes, until they are lightly brown. Remove from the heat and reserve for step 5.

4. Add the remaining ingredients (including the ½ teaspoon salt) to a mixing bowl and blend them with a wooden spoon.

5. Gently incorporate the cooled bread cubes into the flour mixture.

6. Shape the dough into several cylinders measuring 1½ inches in diameter by 3 inches in length.

7. Gently place the dumplings in the boiling water.

8. Adjust the heat to a very low simmer. Cover, and cook for 20 minutes, turning the dumplings halfway through this period.

9. With a slotted spoon, remove the *houskové knedlíky* from the pot, and let them drain briefly. Slice the dumplings into ½-inch-thick disks with a knife or (if you want to be traditional) with a taut piece of string, using a sawing motion. Serve your *houskové knedlíky* immediately.

Additional Keys to Success

If you don't have slightly stale bread, place the cubes made from fresh bread slices on a plate and let stand uncovered at room temperature for at least 12 hours. Alternatively, place the fresh cubes on a cookie sheet in the middle of a preheated 200° F oven for 15 to 20 minutes. ¶ To prevent sticking, moisten your hands before shaping the dumplings. ¶ The dumplings may break apart and will certainly become denser than necessary if cooked at a boil.

Serving Suggestions and Affinities

Overlap the dumpling disks in a ring around the entrée. ¶ Whoever invented *houskové knedlíky* probably had in mind roast goose, duck, or pork. The thick, rich sauce that usually accompanies these entrées brings out the best in the dumplings and is usually spooned over them with abandon.

Variations on a Theme

Omit the baking powder for a firmer, more compact dumpling. ¶ Stuff your *houskové knedlíky* with a medley of chopped mushrooms and onions sautéed in butter. ¶ Wrap the cylindrical dumplings in cheesecloth and steam them over boiling salted water. ¶ Mold the dumplings into balls and cook them in a soup or stew.

◄§ Mamaliga   *Serves 4*
(mah-mah-lee-gah)

Count Dracula the vampire is fictional, of course. The Transylvanian
Alps, on the other hand, are real — and even more beautiful than
Bram Stoker's description of this region in his famous nineteenth-
century novel. Had this English author actually visited the Transylvanian Alps, he probably would have more generously depicted the
breathtaking mountain peaks, peaceful meadows, cozy gabled cottages
with floral designs on their whitewashed walls, and amiable peasants
dressed in their richly embroidered holiday costumes.

Mr. Stoker should have also scribbled a paragraph describing a
peasant preparing *mamaliga,* the bread of Rumania. Basically, *mamaliga*
is a cornmeal mush with sufficient consistency to be sliced with a
knife. It is similar to the Italian peasant specialty of the Po River
valley called *polenta.*

I was given a lesson in making *mamaliga* by a Rumanian peasant
woman in her mountain cottage. She cooked several cups of cornmeal
mixed with water in an oversized cast-iron pot that hung in her fireplace. As her preparation simmered she stirred it with a crudely carved
wooden rod, which she called a *facelet.*

I took charge of the *facelet* midway through the cooking process,
but — to my embarrassment — I had to return the implement to her.
After two minutes of stirring the rapidly thickening mass in the pot,
I was pooped. "You have to develop *mamaliga* muscles," the brawny
cook cracked.

She suggested a practical solution: "Make a smaller batch, as
my daughters and granddaughters do." The following recipe calls
for only one cup of cornmeal, so it shouldn't require "*mamaliga* muscles."

3 cups water	2 tablespoons unsalted butter
½ teaspoon salt (or to taste)	Garnishes (see below)
1 cup yellow cornmeal	

Steps
1. Bring the water and salt to a rapid boil in a large, heavy saucepan.
2. Add the cornmeal in a slow, steady stream, stirring constantly.

3. Cook over low heat for 15 minutes (for fine cornmeal) to 20 minutes (for coarse cornmeal). Stir constantly with a wooden spoon for the first few minutes, then thoroughly stir every minute or two until the cornmeal is cooked.

4. Spoon the *mamaliga* onto a large wooden serving board (or onto a heated flat serving dish).

5. Shape the heap into a smooth, 2-inch-thick symmetrical mound with the back of a moistened wooden spoon.

6. Cut the butter into small pieces and place them on top of the *mamaliga*. Brush the melting butter over the entire surface.

7. Garnish the platter (for ideas, see below).

8. Serve hot. Traditionally, *mamaliga* is cut at the table with a string, using a sawing motion, into ½- to 1-inch-thick breadlike slices.

Additional Keys to Success

Coarse is preferable to fine cornmeal because it has more flavor and, when cooked, a more desirable texture. Coarse cornmeal is available in some Italian and health food stores, or by mail order (see below). Fine cornmeal, such as the Quaker brand, is sold in most supermarkets. ¶ Unless the saucepan is thick-gauged and the heat is low, part of the cornmeal will scorch. ¶ The mixture will lump if the cornmeal is poured into the boiling water too quickly or if you don't constantly stir the mixture during the addition. If the water stops boiling when you are adding the cornmeal, you are incorporating the ingredient too quickly. Should lumps develop, break them up with the spoon as you stir the mixture in step 3. ¶ Caution: As the cornmeal cooks, "minivolcanoes" form on its surface and spew "cornmeal lava." Avoid possible burns by wearing long sleeves. ¶ If the mixture becomes too thick — or, if you have not yet developed *"mamaliga* muscles" for this chore — thin it slightly with some standby boiling water. ¶ When the *mamaliga* stops sticking to the sides of the pan, it is done.

Cold-Water Preparation Method

If you have trouble keeping the cornmeal from lumping and are pre-

pared to sacrifice a little quality, consider using the cold-water preparation method: Soak the cornmeal in 1 cup of cold water for 5 minutes;
then slowly add this mixture to 2 cups of boiling salted water. Proceed
to step 3.

Garnishes

A freshly mounded and buttered *mamaliga* yearns to be crowned and
surrounded by a host of savory and colorful garnishes — the more
the merrier. Popular garnishes include:

Brynza (or feta) cheese
Eggs (poached, fried, or hard-
  cooked)
Grated cheese
Ham, bacon, or sausages
Herb sprigs (dill, parsley, and so
  on)

Olives
Onions, raw or sautéed
Pickles
Roasted red peppers
Sour cream

Serve a light-bodied red wine such as a young Beaujolais.

Serving Variations

Spoon the hot *mamaliga* from the pan directly into a buttered mold,
wait 3 minutes, unmold, and serve. ¶ Spoon the *mamaliga* directly
from the cooking pan to the dinner plate, mashed-potato-style.
¶ Cut the *mamaliga* mound into 1½-inch-thick chunks and top with
meat and its rich sauce. ¶ Cut the *mamaliga* mound into ¾-inch-thick
cubes and gently place them on top of a soup or stew just before
serving. ¶ Slice or cube the *mamaliga* mound and crown the servings
with a garlicky tomato sauce.

Leftovers

Slice room-temperature *mamaliga* and use as the base for an open-
faced sandwich. ¶ Dice room-temperature *mamaliga*, dress the pieces
with vinaigrette, and add chopped parsley and red peppers for color
contrast. ¶ Slice and bread the *mamaliga;* then pan-fry the slabs in
butter. ¶ Cover the *mamaliga* with a sauce of your choice and bake
in a preheated 300° F oven. ¶ Toast garlic-buttered *mamaliga* slices
in the broiler. ¶ Plain *mamaliga* freezes well if tightly wrapped.

Mail-Order Source

Coarse cornmeal is available through the mail from H. Roth & Son, 1577 First Avenue, New York, New York 10028 (212-734-1110).

✑ Papas con Salsa Queso   *Serves 4*
(PAH-pahs cohn SAHL-sah KEH-soh)

One of the most unforgettable days of my life occurred in 1968 in Peru. Because the other six overnight guests at the local hotel had chosen to sleep late, I had Machu Picchu — the lost city of the Incas — to myself. For a few precious hours, starting at dawn, I was able to explore in serene solitude the terraces and well-kept ruins of this breathtaking Inca hideaway.

By late morning the sleepyheads had awakened and the hordes of day trippers were arriving on the excursion train from Cuzco. Not wanting to see Machu Picchu with tourists swarming over it like ants, I left the ruins and wandered down a steep path to a small village on the Urubamba River, two thousand feet below.

My good fortune continued when I met a peasant woman, dressed in the traditional black bowler hat and colorful shawl of the region. She taught me how to make *papas con salsa queso* ("potatoes with cheese"). Potatoes, of course, are very much a part of this land — they were cultivated here in prehistoric times, long before they were ever planted in the potato belts of Idaho, Ireland, and Germany.

3 quarts water
3 teaspoons salt
1 tablespoon annatto seeds
12 small to medium-sized boiling potatoes
⅔ cup finely crumbled *queso blanco* cheese

2 tablespoons minced fresh green chili pepper
1 tablespoon lard
¼ cup chopped white onions
1 teaspoon lime (or lemon) juice

Steps

1. Bring the water and salt to a boil in a 5- to 6-quart pot.
2. Place the annatto seeds in a small heat-proof bowl. Ladle ½ cup of the boiling water over the seeds. Reserve for step 6.
3. Boil the potatoes in their skins for 20 to 25 minutes, or until their cores can be easily pierced with the point of a sharp knife.
4. Purée the cheese and chili, using a mortar and pestle — or a food processor or electric blender. Strain the annatto seed liquid into the cheese mixture (discard the seeds). Thoroughly blend the ingredients.
5. Melt the lard in a heavy-bottomed, 1- to 2-quart saucepan over low to moderate heat. Sauté the onions for 2 minutes, stirring frequently.
6. Reduce the heat to low and stir in the cheese purée. Stir the mixture frequently as you cook it for 5 minutes, or until the sauce begins to thicken.
7. Drain the cooked potatoes while the sauce is cooking in step 6. Peel the potatoes and arrange them on a warm serving platter.
8. Stir the lime juice into the sauce. Spoon the sauce on top of the potatoes. Serve immediately.

Additional Keys to Success

If annatto seeds are unavailable, give your sauce its characteristic reddish-yellow hue with a combination of tomatoes and turmeric. You won't have the same flavor, however. ¶ If you can't purchase *queso blanco* cheese, substitute a fifty-fifty mixture of cottage cheese and a mild soft cheese such as Monterey jack. ¶ Substitute a fifty-fifty blend of vegetable oil and butter for the lard, if necessary. ¶ Adjust the quantity of chili according to your built-up immunity to that spice — but, remember, the sauce is supposed to be hot. ¶ If you cook the sauce at too high a temperature or if you don't stir it frequently in steps 6 and 8, the cheese may curdle. When you add the lime juice (an acid) to the sauce in step 8, the vulnerability to curdling markedly increases.

Serving Suggestions

Papas con salsa queso can be presented as a starch side dish or as a light evening snack. This recipe can also serve three people as a meatless main dish.

Variations on a Theme

Enrich the sauce with milk or cream. ¶ Serve the potatoes unpeeled. ¶ Garnish the sauced potatoes with chopped parsley, slivered hot or sweet peppers, crumbled hard-cooked egg whites, or thinly sliced black olives. ¶ On hot days, serve the sauce over chilled potatoes.

Mail-Order Source

Annatto seeds and turmeric are available through the mail from H. Roth & Son, 1577 First Avenue, New York, New York 10028 (212-734-1110).

✑ Speckknödel
(sphek-k'NOY-duhl)

Serves 3 to 4

Speckknödel, dumplings emboldened with bacon and heavy cream, are laden with calories. Austrian Tyrolean peasants, who live in a region bounded by Germany to the north and Italy and Switzerland to the south, require this type of energy-rich food. Farming and cattle herding in the thin mountain air of the Alps is demanding and laborious.

The Austrian Tyroleans are, for the most part, German-speaking and followers of the Roman Catholic faith. Their homeland lies completely within the grandeur of the Alps. Some Tyroleans I met live at elevations of up to six thousand feet in isolated farmhouses or in tightly clustered minivillages on the sunny side of the steep Alpine slopes. At lower elevations, others dwell in fertile valleys — or along the banks of serene mountain lakes surrounded by dense forests still roamed by deer, bears, and wolves. The refreshing scent of pines, birches, and beeches is everywhere.

Traditional Tyrolean country houses, like their counterparts in most other parts of the Alps, resemble oversized cuckoo clocks, complete with low-pitched roofs and weathered wooden balconies featuring scalloped borders. Inside, the kitchens are warmed by old-fashioned wood stoves.

6 slices slightly stale white bread
5 slices thick-cut bacon
⅓ cup light cream
½ cup flour
½ teaspoon baking powder
Heaping ¼ teaspoon caraway
  seeds
¼ teaspoon dried thyme
¼ teaspoon freshly ground black
  pepper

½ teaspoon salt (or to taste)
Yolk of 1 large egg
1 tablespoon unsalted butter
½ cup sliced white onions
½ pound rinsed and drained
  sauerkraut
1 tablespoon chopped fresh
  parsley

Steps

1. Trim the bread slices and cut them into ½-inch cubes.
2. Cut the bacon slices into ⅓-inch squares. Sauté them over moderate heat in a large skillet for about 5 minutes. Stir frequently. Transfer them to paper towels with a slotted spoon, and pat dry.
3. Pour water to a depth of 3 inches into a wide-bottomed pot and bring it to a simmer (in preparation for step 8).
4. Brown the bread cubes in the hot bacon fat for 3 to 5 minutes. Transfer them to a large bowl.
5. Add the cream to the bowl. Gently toss the bread until it absorbs all the cream. Add to this mixture the bacon, flour, baking powder, caraway seeds, thyme, pepper, and ¼ teaspoon of the salt. Beat the egg yolk and add it to the bowl. Gently blend the ingredients.
6. Shape the mixture into 1¼-inch spheres with your hands. (If your mixture is too dry, moisten it with a little more cream.) Place the dumplings on a plate as you make them, arranging them in one layer so they do not touch each other.
7. Melt the butter over low to moderate heat in a clean large skillet. Add the onions and sauté for 2 minutes. Add the sauerkraut and the remaining salt and blend the mixture. Cover, and cook for 12 minutes.
8. Cook the dumplings in the simmering water for about 10 minutes (start this step as soon as you cover the onion-sauerkraut pan). You need not turn the dumplings; they will do that by themselves.
9. Transfer the cooked *speckknödel* to a warm bowl and cover them with the onion-sauerkraut mixture. Garnish with the parsley and serve immediately.

Additional Keys to Success

Purchase a top-quality, well-smoked bacon. ¶ If you don't have slightly stale bread, place the cubes made from fresh bread slices on a plate and let stand uncovered at room temperature for at least 12 hours. Alternatively, place the fresh cubes on a cookie sheet in the middle of a preheated 200° F oven for 15 to 20 minutes. ¶ If your caraway seeds are old (and therefore exceptionally dry), soak them in water for 30 minutes before adding them in step 5. ¶ To prevent sticking, moisten your hands with water before shaping the dumplings.

Affinities

Beer is the traditional beverage accompaniment. A dry, medium-bodied white wine is a good choice, too, if it is assertive enough to stand up to the onion-sauerkraut topping.

Variations on a Theme

Serve your *speckknödel* on a bed of — rather than under — the onion-sauerkraut mixture. ¶ Substitute for the onion-sauerkraut topping a generous sprinkling of grated cheese or a ladling of meat gravy. In either case, incorporate sautéed onions into the dumpling mixture. ¶ Cook the dumplings in a meat stock. ¶ Cook and serve the dumplings in a soup or stew.

Mail-Order Source

Caraway seeds are available through the mail from H. Roth & Son, 1577 First Avenue, New York, New York 10028 (212-734-1110).

✎ Tabbouleh   *Serves 4*
(tah-ʙoo-lay)

On the narrow Mediterranean coastal plain of Lebanon sits Tyre, once a proud and impenetrable Phoenician island-city that withstood a thirteen-year siege in the sixth century ʙ.ᴄ. by Nebuchadnezzar, king of Babylonia. His army was unable to scale the imposing 150-

foot-high stone walls of Tyre, because it could not safely transport its ponderous siege engines across an exposed strait a third of a mile wide.

In 333 B.C., Alexander arrived, determined not to suffer the same fate as Nebuchadnezzar. He had a dream that suggested he could link the island to the mainland by constructing a causeway. He did, and the "impregnable" Tyre tasted bitter defeat.

Today, the causeway — Alexander's dream come true — still exists, though in a much expanded form. The drifting sands of time have broadened this raised path and the needs of man have sprinkled it with dwellings, including the house of a fisherman I had met while exploring the harbor of Tyre. He invited me to his home to show me how his family prepares the popular bulgur wheat-based *tabbouleh.*

"We make our own bulgur wheat," he said proudly. His wife led me up the stairwell to the roof, where parboiled whole wheat grains were drying on a cloth spread out under the dazzling sun. She gathered a small bucketful and returned to her kitchen. She cracked the wheat berries in a grinder to a fine degree of coarseness, and then proceeded with this recipe.

2 cups fine-grained bulgur
1 cup thinly sliced scallions
1 cup chopped fresh mint
¼ teaspoon cinnamon
½ teaspoon salt (or to taste)

1½ cups chopped ripe tomatoes
½ cup fresh lemon juice
⅔ cup olive oil
Lettuce leaves

Steps

1. Cover the bulgur with a 2-inch-deep layer of cold water in a deep, noncorrosible bowl. Soak it for 1 hour at room temperature.
2. Drain the bulgur well.
3. Add the scallions, mint, cinnamon, salt, tomatoes, lemon juice, and olive oil. Gently toss the ingredients until they are well blended. Refrigerate the *tabbouleh* for at least 3 hours.
4. Toss the *tabbouleh* gently. Serve it in a mound on top of a single layer of lettuce leaves in a bowl, on a serving platter, or on individual plates.

Additional Keys to Success

Depending on your taste, use only the white portion, or both the white and lower part of the green portions, of the scallions. ❡ If fresh mint is not available, substitute ⅔ cup of chopped parsley plus 2 tablespoons of dried crumbled mint. ❡ For a peasant-style *tabbouleh*, do not chop the mint and tomatoes too finely. ❡ For optimum flavor, use a good brand of virgin olive oil. ❡ Step 3 is necessary so that the ingredients can blend their flavors and create new ones.

Serving Suggestions and Affinities

Use a glass serving bowl or dish. ❡ *Tabbouleh* is at its glorious best during the warm-weather months. ❡ Serve it as an appetizer, salad, or side dish. ❡ *Tabbouleh* is a sure-fire party dish. ❡ Use pita bread pieces as "edible spoons" to scoop up the *tabbouleh*.   ❡ Alternatively, place a dollop of *tabbouleh* on top of a lettuce leaf. Roll the lettuce taco-style and eat the treat with your fingers.

Variations on a Theme

Experiment with medium-grained bulgur. ❡ Substitute mace, cloves, or cardamom for the cinnamon. ❡ Add other ingredients, such as diced cucumber and Italian pepper. ❡ For a softer-textured *tabbouleh*, cover the bulgur with boiling rather than cold water, and reduce the soaking time to 30 minutes.

Leftovers

Consider doubling the recipe, because *tabbouleh* develops new and subtle flavors as it sits in the refrigerator for two or three days.

Mail-Order Sources

Fine-grained and medium-grained bulgur are available through the mail from Karnig Tashjian, 380 Third Avenue, New York, New York 10016 (212-683-8458). Mace and cardamom are available from H. Roth & Son, 1577 First Avenue, New York, New York 10028 (212-734-1110).

Other
Specialties ❧

❦ Äppelkaka   *Serves 4 to 6*
(EHP-pell-KAH-gah)

Swedes pay homage in late June to the arrival of the longest day of the year. They greet it somewhat red-eyed, the result of staying up all night partaking in the annual Midsummer Eve Celebration.

Maypoles are erected in village squares and the residents and countryfolk come to sing, fiddle, dance, eat, drink, and laugh through the "night." I place this last word in quotes because at these latitudes at this time of year there is no darkness. The sky lingers in a state of twilight in the sparse hours between sunrise and sunset. If you happen to be above the Arctic Circle, the sun rotates around the horizon, never setting at all. This is one of the eeriest, most disconcerting phenomena I've ever experienced.

I attended a Midsummer Eve Celebration in Dalarna, a region of central Sweden noted for its beautiful lakes, forests, and maidens. Fishing, too, is outstanding. During the festivities I enjoyed a perfectly grilled brook char freshly caught in a nearby swift mountain stream. I finished my meal with one of the country's most beloved desserts: *äppelkaka.*

"Swedish apple cake" is not really a cake in the English sense of that term. In Sweden, *äppelkaka* is a soft, delectable mass comprising alternating layers of applesauce and bread crumbs.

I accompanied my *äppelkaka* with a cup of coffee, Sweden's national nonalcoholic drink. It was strong and black, as Swedes prefer it. Swedish-style coffee and *äppelkaka* are as natural an affinity as you are likely to find.

⅓ cup water
1½ pounds tart apples
⅓ cup light brown sugar

½ teaspoon allspice
5 tablespoons unsalted butter
1 cup zwieback crumbs

177

Steps

1. Preheat the oven to 350° F.
2. Bring the water to a boil in a 2-quart saucepan.
3. Peel, cut into eighths, and core the apples. Stir the sugar and allspice into the boiling water. Add the apples and coat them thoroughly with the liquid. Cover, and simmer over low to moderate heat for 6 to 8 minutes, stirring occasionally. Break up the apples with a wooden spoon or potato masher to form a pulpy sauce.
4. Melt 4 tablespoons of the butter in a medium-sized skillet. Add the zwieback crumbs and sauté them over medium heat for several minutes, until lightly brown. Stir constantly.
5. Grease an oven-proof dish (approximately 3 cups capacity) with ½ tablespoon of the remaining butter.
6. Arrange several alternating layers of crumbs and applesauce, starting and ending with the crumbs. The crumb layers should be approximately ⅛ inch thick and the applesauce layers about ⅓ inch thick.
7. Dot the top of the *äppelkaka* with the remaining ½ tablespoon of butter.
8. Bake the *äppelkaka* for 25 minutes.
9. Remove the *äppelkaka* from the oven and cool to room temperature.
10. Slice the *äppelkaka* into individual portions and serve each piece with a topping of your choice (see below).

Additional Keys to Success

The apples must be firm and tart. Best bets include Rome Beauty, Rhode Island Greening, and York Imperial. Above all, never use a Red or Golden Delicious. ¶ If you do not have zwieback crumbs, use rye or — if necessary — unseasoned standard bread crumbs. ¶ Whatever your choice of bread crumbs, be sure they are dry and coarse-textured. ¶ For a firmer-textured *äppelkaka*, refrigerate it overnight (after baking).

Topping Suggestions

One popular topping is whipped cream flavored with sugar and vanilla. Others include chilled cream; vanilla custard; ice cream. *Äppelkaka* is a delight by itself, too.

Mail-Order Source

Zwieback is available through the mail from Bremen House, 220 East 86th Street, New York, New York 10028 (212-288-5500).

✑ Blackberry Fool   *Serves 4*

I've long wondered how the English dessert "fool" received its curious name. I put the question to a Devonshire farmer. "You're the fool if you worry about things like that when all you have to do is to sit down and enjoy it," he quipped. He had a point.

Before I could pamper myself with this thick purée of fresh fruits blended with whipped cream, there was the matter of collecting the ingredients. My farmer acquaintance and I strolled down a country lane near his house, through a patchwork of pastures framed by hedgerows. Partially hidden within these leafy walls were berries growing wild. The blackberries were the ripest, so we picked them one by one, dropping the fruit into a wicker basket until we had gathered a pint.

We returned to the farmhouse with our treasure and prepared the fruit purée. Meanwhile, the farmer's wife sauntered out to the barn to milk the family's cow. Fifteen minutes later she carried the day's yield of milk to the kitchen, where it separated into milk and cream. Before the sun set I was enjoying the freshest fool I had ever eaten.

Devonshire is famous for its dairy products — cream, butter, cheese, and clotted cream. It is also a land of splendid rustic beauty. Between its two rugged coastlines are landscapes sure to please the eye of any professional photographer. Cozy thatched cottages and lilliputian villages with storybook names are nestled among the undulating hills, as are farms, dairies, orchards, forests, and high granite outcroppings called tors. Don't miss Devonshire the next time you're in England.

1 pint blackberries	6 tablespoons sugar
2 teaspoons water	1 cup heavy cream

Steps
1. Wash and stem the blackberries.
2. Add the water and the fruit to a 1½- to 2-quart heavy-bottomed saucepan. Slightly mash the berries with a wooden spoon. Cover, and cook over low heat for 5 minutes. Blend in the sugar. Cover, and cook for an additional 15 minutes, stirring and crushing occasionally.
3. Cool the mixture and refrigerate it for at least 2 hours.
4. Whip the cream to the stiff-peak stage.
5. Fold the fruit mixture into the whipped cream.
6. Spoon the fool into individual parfait or sherbet glasses. Alternatively, transfer the fool to a 1-quart crystal bowl. Serve immediately or, if the day is particularly hot, refrigerate the fool for about 2 hours.

Additional Keys to Success
If you overcrush, overcook, or sieve the blackberries, you won't have a country-style fool. ¶ Whip the cream in a well-chilled bowl. ¶ Do not overfold the fruit into the whipped cream. The fool should be mottled with white and blackberry tones. ¶ Chill the serving glasses or bowl.

Variations on a Theme
Substitute such other fruits as gooseberries (the classic fool), cloudberries, raspberries, strawberries, red or black currants, and crab apples. Adjust the sugar in keeping with the natural tartness and ripeness of the fruit. If the fruit has relatively large seeds, you must sieve it. ¶ Some chefs omit the cooking step for fruits that can normally be eaten out of hand (strawberries, for instance). ¶ Modern recipes sometimes switch custard for the whipped cream.

⤚§ Chae
(chy)

Serves 4

The road that cuts through the historic Khyber Pass connects Afghanistan and Pakistan, from Jalalabad to Fort Jamrud on the vast Peshawar Plain. A few conquering armies from central Asia have fought their way through these steep series of gorges on their way to the riches of India. Most armies failed because the Khyber Pass was so narrow in sections that a traveler with outstretched arms could practically touch the facing cliffs. Before these bottlenecks were dynamited to make way for the modern two-lane road, a small band of determined defenders could easily halt an enemy's progress.

My trip through the Khyber Pass was peaceful and rewarding. I came upon several mud-brick houses enclosed within a thick adobe wall guarded by squat towers with crumbling battlements. The head man of the compound brought me inside and shared his simple meal: a flat loaf of whole-wheat *nan* bread still warm from the clay oven, and a pot of steaming *chae* (tea) enlivened with fragrant spices.

He was a member of one of the Pathan tribes, and his features and dress manifested it. He was tall in stature and upright in bearing. The sun had tanned his fair skin, which set off his blue eyes — not unusual for a Pathan. Under his aquiline nose he sported a fierce black mustache. He wore a striped vest, and a long and dark cotton shirt over his baggy white trousers; he graced his head with a carefully wrapped turban and adorned his feet with pointed soft leather shoes.

Against the wall leaned his lengthy rifle. He carried it strapped on his back whenever he ventured beyond the compound, because his family, I was told, had an ongoing feud with another clan dating back two hundred years. Pathans are so quick to take insult and slow to forget the affront that they make the Hatfields and McCoys seem like kissing cousins. Fortunately, these Afghans are also noted for their hospitality — and for their invigorating spiced tea.

1 quart water
4 teaspoons black tea
Seeds of 1 cardamom pod
1 3-inch cinnamon stick

½ teaspoon whole coriander
   seeds
1 whole clove

Steps

1. Bring the water to a boil.
2. Put the tea leaves and all the spices in a warm teapot. Pour in the boiling water. Do not stir the liquid.
3. Cover the teapot and let the tea brew undisturbed for 5 minutes.
4. Give the brew a few gentle stirs. Pour it through a strainer into warm teacups.

Additional Keys to Success

In step 1, boil cold tap water. Hot tap water usually has acquired some of the taste of the hot water pipes and boiler. ¶ Don't let the water boil for more than a minute or two. As water boils, it loses oxygen and therefore begins to taste flat. ¶ For better flavor, use loose tea leaves. If you must use tea bags, remember that one tea bag is the approximate equivalent of 1 teaspoon of loose tea. ¶ If you have only ground spices, substitute 2 pinches of cardamom, 1 generous pinch each of coriander seed and cinnamon, and 1 meager pinch of cloves. ¶ By not stirring the leaves in the liquid in step 2, and by giving the liquid no more than a few lazy stirs in step 4, you minimize the bitter flavor that will be extracted from the tea leaves.

Variations on a Theme

Experiment with other aromatic spices such as nutmeg and ginger. ¶ Some Afghans add sugar to their tea.

Mail-Order Source

Cardamom pods, cinnamon sticks, coriander seeds, whole cloves, and ginger are available through the mail from H. Roth & Son, 1577 First Avenue, New York, New York 10028 (212-734-1110).

⋖⋗ Kissel
(kee-SUHL)

Serves 4

The Soviet Union is the largest nation on earth, and I could spend a lifetime exploring it. "To grasp the vastness of this country, look at the full moon," I remember my high-school geography teacher lecturing. "The USSR is greater in area than the half of the moon we see."

Dominating the European quarter of the Soviet Union are flat, rolling, endless steppes. They consist mainly of grassy plains, virgin forests, and — as in the environs of Moscow — collective farms.

On one of these collective farms, a peasant cook taught me how to make *kissel*. If you exclude ice cream, *kissel* is the most popular dessert of the Russians (it's also a favorite in the Balkans, Poland, and parts of Scandinavia). *Kissel* is a sweetened fruit purée thickened to a jellylike consistency with cornstarch or potato flour. It is traditionally served in a glass cup and topped with cream or custard.

I noticed that many Russians use an instant *kissel* product, but not my mentor cook. The difference between her freshly made *kissel* and the packaged version was like the difference between a brash note and a subtle one. Since it's so simple to make *kissel* the old-fashioned way, I wonder why any serious cook would bother with the convenience product.

1 pint fresh raspberries	2 tablespoons cornstarch
½ cup sugar	⅓ cup heavy cream
1½ cups plus 2 tablespoons water	

Steps

1. Wash and stem the raspberries.
2. Place the fruit, sugar, and 1½ cups of water in a 1½- to 2-quart saucepan, and bring to a boil. Reduce the heat to a low simmer and cook the mixture, uncovered, for 12 minutes. Stir occasionally.
3. Strain the mixture through a fine sieve set over another saucepan. Bring the liquid to a boil.
4. Put the cornstarch into a small bowl and thoroughly blend in the 2 tablespoons of water.

5. Dissolve the cornstarch slurry in the raspberry liquid. Reduce the heat to a low simmer. Stirring constantly, cook the liquid for about 3 minutes, or until it starts to thicken.

6. Let the liquid cool slightly and then pour it into individual glass dessert dishes. Refrigerate the *kissel* for several hours or overnight.

7. Pour a ⅛- to ¼-inch-thick layer of heavy cream over the chilled and solidified *kissel*. Serve immediately.

Additional Keys to Success

Unless the raspberries are perfectly ripe, you may have to add a little more sugar to keep the acidity and sweetness in balance. ¶ To keep the *kissel* from becoming too cloudy, do not exert more than moderate pressure when you are sieving the mixture in step 3.

Variations on a Theme

Kissel can be served hot as a fruit sauce. ¶ Prepare a two-layered dessert of custard on the bottom and *kissel* on top (make and chill the custard; then concoct the *kissel* layer). ¶ Reserve some of the whole raspberries and add them to the dessert dish just before you pour in the *kissel*. ¶ Substitute another tart fruit such as blackberries, currants, cranberries, or strawberries for the raspberries. Or use tart cherries or apples.

↜ Pan Bagna   *Serves 4*
(pahn bahn'YA)

On a sunny midafternoon in June I was hiking through the hilly countryside behind Cannes. It was a day to rejoice. The Mediterranean sky was bright and cheery. Around me small birds darted back and forth from bush to bush through the warm Provençal air scented by wild thyme and sage. Along the way I met a farmer mending his stone fence. After the exchange of a few pleasantries, I offered him some of the wine I had stored in my knapsack. He in turn gave me half his *pan bagna*.

Never before had a sandwich tasted so wonderful. Some of my friends have suggested that my fondness for the *pan bagna* was due to my hunger, or to the effect of the herb-scented breeze. I'm convinced that *pan bagna* is one irresistible sandwich wherever you happen to be eating it.

Pan bagna is popular throughout most of Provence with peasants and rich folks alike. Workers take it into the vineyards, families stuff it into picnic baskets, and vendors hawk it along stretches of the French Riviera to topless sun goddesses.

Pan bagna can survive for several hours outside the refrigerator in the summer principally because the vinegar inhibits the growth of harmful microorganisms. With so many scorching days in Provence, the sandwich has an obvious place in the regional culinary scene. Another defense against spoiling is its goodness — a well-made *pan bagna* doesn't sit around too long before it is devoured by a two-legged mammal.

1 large loaf French bread	4 pitted black olives
⅓ cup olive oil	2 scallions
2 tablespoons vinegar	8 medium-sized capers
4 medium-sized mushrooms	2 hard-cooked large eggs
2 medium-sized tomatoes	6 anchovy fillets
2 cornichons	Lettuce

Steps

1. Slice the loaf in half lengthwise as you would a hot dog bun.
2. Brush (or sprinkle) the olive oil and the vinegar on the cut surface of both halves.
3. Slice the mushrooms and arrange them on the cut surface of the bottom half of the loaf.
4. Slice the tomatoes and arrange them on top of the mushrooms.
5. Slice the cornichons, olives, and the white portion of the scallions. Chop the capers. Arrange these ingredients on the tomato layer.
6. Slice the eggs and arrange them on top of the other ingredients.
7. Cut the anchovies into eighths and place them on top of the eggs.
8. Cover the top layer with two layers of lettuce.
9. Cover the lettuce with the top half of the loaf. Seal the *pan bagna* in plastic wrap and weight it down (with about 10 pounds of books, pans, or other appropriate objects) at room temperature for about 1 hour.

10. Unwrap the *pan bagna* and slice it crosswise into four sandwiches. Serve promptly.

Additional Keys to Success

A proper *pan bagna* is liberally drenched with olive oil; so don't cut down on that ingredient. ¶ For flavor's sake, use a good brand of imported virgin olive oil.

Serving Suggestions and Affinities

Accompany your *pan bagna* with cheese, preferably one made from goat's or ewe's milk. ¶ Drink a well-chilled, dry rosé wine — or an ice-cold beer.

Variations on a Theme

Rub the interior surface of the bread with crushed garlic before beginning step 2. ¶ If you can't find cornichons, substitute gherkins (similar to cornichons but sweeter). ¶ Eliminate the anchovies (if you do, give the egg layer a light sprinkling of salt). ¶ Experiment with other ingredients such as tuna, sliced Italian peppers, and artichoke hearts. ¶ *Pan bagna* can be made with crusty bread rolls.

Mail-Order Source

Cornichons are available through the mail from H. Roth & Son, 1577 First Avenue, New York, New York 10028 (212-734-1110).

◄§ Pesto   *Makes approximately ⅝ cup*
(PEH-stoh)

A handful of fishing villages repose under the majestic sea cliffs that dominate the rocky Ligurian coastline of northwest Italy, which stretches from France to Tuscany. Some of these are reached best by boat — the narrow paths that zigzag down the cliffs are used only by sure-footed climbers, mules, and goats, and certainly not by people like me who are hampered with mild cases of acrophobia.

I've visited some of these isolated villages in Cinqueterre, one hundred miles south of Genoa. Its name translates as "five lands."

Cinqueterre wine is a conversation piece among wine aficionados. It is the only domestic wine vinted in mainland Italy that must be shipped by sea before it can be sipped in a café along the Via Veneto in Rome. Soon this delightful aspect of Cinqueterre wine will come to an end — the government, I've been told, is planning to build a road linking the villages to the country's highway system.

I was taught how to make *pesto* in one of the villages of Cinqueterre by a woman who had a limitless supply of basil growing in crude terraces behind her stucco house. On command, her daughter darted out the back door, scampered up the hill, and gathered a basketful of basil. The young girl believed that hers was the finest basil on earth, and I had no reason to dispute her claim.

Her mother separated the leaves and placed them with some garlic in a marble mortar. She picked up the pestle (the words *pesto* and *pestle* have a common Latin ancestor) and ground her ingredients into a coarse paste. After crushing the pine nuts and grated cheese into her mixture, she slowly blended in some olive oil. Before my eyes she transformed the five ingredients into *pesto,* the pungent green sauce of Liguria that is usually used with pasta.

2 loosely packed cups stemmed fresh basil	⅓ cup freshly grated Parmesan cheese
3 medium-sized garlic cloves	¼ to ⅜ cup olive oil
3 tablespoons pine nuts	

Mortar and Pestle Steps

1. Add the basil leaves and garlic to the mortar and pound the mixture with the pestle into a coarse paste.
2. Add the pine nuts and cheese and pound them into the mixture.
3. Add the olive oil 2 tablespoons at a time. Blend briefly after each addition. Stop adding the olive oil when the consistency reaches the coarse paste stage (*pesto* should not be a liquidy purée).

Food Processor Steps

1. Mince the garlic as finely as possible in a food processor, using the steel blade. Scrape down the sides of the bowl as necessary. Alternatively, finely mince the garlic on a chopping board before adding it to the bowl.

2. Add the basil leaves, pine nuts, and cheese to the bowl. Turning the machine on and off quickly, chop the leaves to a coarse texture, scraping down the sides of the bowl as necessary.

3. Pour in the olive oil in a steady stream while you quickly turn the machine on and off about half a dozen times. Periodically scrape down the sides. Stop adding the oil when the consistency reaches the coarse paste stage (pesto should not be a liquidy purée).

Additional Keys to Success

Use a well-aged cheese (ask your cheesemonger for several-year-old Parmigiano Reggiano). ¶ *Pesto* tastes better if it is allowed to stand at room temperature for 1 hour before serving.

Serving Suggestions and Affinities

Estimate 2 to 3 tablespoons of *pesto* per serving of pasta. ¶ Ligurians also use *pesto* to flavor their local version of minestrone. ¶ Use your *pesto* for *gnocchi,* baked squash or potatoes, or sliced fresh tomatoes. Fish, too, can benefit from a dollop of *pesto.*

Variations on a Theme

If available, use Sardo, the pungent ewe's milk cheese from Sardinia. Or, use a fifty-fifty blend of Parmesan and Sardo or Pecorino Romano. ¶ Some chefs add other ingredients such as cream, salt, and pepper (though I never saw a Ligurian peasant who did).

Leftovers

Place the *pesto* in a glass jar. Pack it down and cover it with a layer of olive oil. Thus stored, it will last for at least several weeks in the refrigerator or for a couple of months in the freezer. For longer freezing periods, do not add the garlic, cheese, or pine nuts — incorporate these ingredients into the olive oil and basil mixture when you thaw it.

Mail-Order Source

Pine nuts are available through the mail from Karnig Tashjian, 380 Third Avenue, New York, New York 10016 (212-683-8458).

✑§ Raclette
(rah-KLET)

Serves 4

The most spectacular Alpine scenery of Switzerland is in the French-speaking canton of Valais, site of the Matterhorn and other soaring peaks. Tucked away within the lofty mountain terrain are remote valleys where the incessant sound of ringing cowbells mingles with the whistling winds. These high-lying valleys are used for pasturage in the summer, when the grass is green and plentiful. Come fall, the cows are herded down to warmer meadows situated near the year-round, chalet-style farmhouses of the Swiss dairymen.

In one of these dwellings lived a family I had met while skiing on a bright February Sunday morn. They invited me to their snow-covered home to enjoy *raclette*, the melted-cheese specialty of Valais.

My host fetched from his cellar a hunk of cheese made from the milk of his cows. As he propped the cheese on top of a large stone in front of the fireplace, he explained to me the ritual of eating *raclette*.

"Once the surface of the cheese begins to melt," he said, "pick up one of the plates I've laid near the fire. Take turns with the rest of us in scraping off some of the cheese onto your plate." *Raclette*, I learned later, derives from the French word *racler*, meaning "to scrape."

Following my host's lead, I also placed on my plate some of the tidbits — including boiled potatoes — that he had arranged on a side table. I spread some of the cheese on the potatoes, seasoned them with freshly ground black pepper, and in between bites took nibbles of cornichons and pickled pearl onions. By the time we had finished our first round, the surface of the cheese had once again melted; so we had seconds and then thirds.

Though *raclette* is served in both elegant urban restaurants and humble rustic homes, it seems to taste best in the latter. *Raclette* needs a cozy, homey environment.

12 small new potatoes	Cornichons
1 2-pound wedge Raclette cheese	Pickled pearl onions
	Freshly ground black pepper

Steps

1. Place the unpeeled potatoes in boiling salted water (1 teaspoon of salt per quart of liquid) and reduce the heat to a simmer. Cook for 18 to 22 minutes, depending on the thickness of the potatoes.
2. Warm the serving plates.
3. Drain the potatoes and keep them warm in a fire-proof container near the fire.
4. Remove the rind from the cheese. Place the cheese on a fire-proof platter about 1 foot in front of the fire. Face the largest cut side toward the heat.
5. Follow the traditional eating ritual described in the introduction to this recipe.

Raclette Cheese

Raclette cheese is imported into this country. If you can't find any, substitute the equally suitable Bagnes or Gomser cheeses from the Valais region. Cheeses of slightly less suitability are Appenzeller, Gruyère, and Emmentaler, the genuine "Swiss cheese." Whatever the cheese, it should be reasonably mild, semisoft, and creamy, and it should have good melting qualities.

Cornichons

Cornichons are small, sour pickles and are available in jars in many gourmet food stores. If they are unavailable, use American-style gherkins, which are similar to cornichons but much sweeter.

Pickled Pearl Onions

These onions are usually sold in jars under the name "cocktail onions."

Wine

The most traditional wine for *raclette* is Fendant, a dry white from Valais. However, almost any decent, dry, medium-bodied white wine will do. So will a dry, light-bodied red such as a Beaujolais. Alternatively, sip a glass of kirschwasser or beer.

Additional Keys to Success

You generally require only ¼ pound of cheese per person, but this recipe suggests 2 pounds for four people because a smaller piece generally doesn't keep its shape as well in front of the fire. Save the leftover cheese for another use. ¶ The cheese melts more uniformly if it is on the same level as the center of the heat source. Therefore, place the platter of cheese in front of the fire on an ad hoc elevated platform made of bricks or cement blocks. ¶ Unless the serving plates are warm, the scraped cheese will prematurely cool and solidify. ¶ Conclude your *raclette* party with a bowl of mixed fresh fruits laced with kirschwasser.

Variations on a Theme

Raclette can also be prepared with special table-top ovens (however, these modern gadgets never create the feeling of a genuine *raclette* party held in front of a fireplace). ¶ Though it's not traditional, you can also serve sliced cucumbers, radishes, butter, and crusty French bread.

Mail-Order Source

Cornichons are available through the mail from H. Roth & Son, 1577 First Avenue, New York, New York 10028 (212-734-1110).

✍§ Soda Bread   *Makes 1 round loaf*

"It's a long way to Tipperary," the international hit song advises us. This county and town of Ireland may be a respectable distance from America, but not from most parts of the Emerald Isle. It took me only several leisurely hours to drive from Dublin to Tipperary — and transit time hardly mattered to me because I traveled through verdant, moderately pitching hills dotted with the ruins of thirteenth-century abbeys and castle keeps.

County Tipperary is dairy and cattle-raising land, one of inspiring beauty for any Irish poet. Wherever you turn your eye you see fertile green fields crisscrossed by crude stone walls and sprinkled with white-washed thatched cottages.

Inside many of these farmhouses the women go through the daily routine of preparing soda bread for their families. Because this delicious specialty is quick and easy to make, I would scarcely call it a chore. I've seen many a cook bake her bread the old-fashioned way: A round of dough rests in a covered cast-iron pot hung over a bed of slow-burning peat, the traditional cooking fuel of Ireland. By nightfall, peat perfumes the countryside with its unmistakable pungent scent and the families inside their homes sit down to a meal that almost always features freshly made soda bread.

2 cups whole-wheat flour	2 teaspoons baking soda
2 cups white flour	1¾ cups buttermilk
¾ teaspoon salt (or to taste)	½ teaspoon unsalted butter

Steps

1. Preheat the oven to 375° F.
2. Mix the flours, salt, and baking soda in a bowl.
3. Make a well in the center of the dry ingredients. Gradually pour the buttermilk into the crater while stirring with a wooden spoon. Thoroughly mix the ingredients.
4. Knead the dough on a lightly floured board (or in the mixing bowl) for several minutes.
5. Shape the dough into a flat round loaf approximately 1½ inches high by 8 inches in diameter.
6. Grease a baking sheet with the butter.
7. Place the shaped dough on the sheet.
8. Divide the top surface into quadrants by cutting a ½-inch-deep X across the loaf. Use a sharp knife.
9. Place the sheet on the middle rack of the oven and bake for 35 to 40 minutes.
10. Place your Irish soda bread on a cooling rack for about 5 minutes before serving.

Additional Keys to Success

You will have to use a little more buttermilk if your flours are drier than usual (as would be the case if they have been stored for a long time). ¶ Work quickly from steps 3 to 9. Otherwise, too much of the leavening power created by combining the buttermilk and baking soda will be dissipated before the dough enters the oven. ¶ The dough will stick less to your hands if you lightly flour them before starting to knead. ¶ The bread is done as soon as it sounds hollow when tapped. ¶ If you don't place the baked bread on top of a cooling rack or other grate, the bottom will not be crisp.

Variations on a Theme

Some recipes specify that the flour be exclusively white. Though an all-white-flour bread will have a lighter texture, it will not be as nutritious or authentic as the Irish soda bread made with a combination of white and whole-wheat flours. Yet other recipes call for such untraditional ingredients as sugar, baking powder, and shortening. ¶ For a soft crust, swathe the bread in a kitchen towel immediately upon removing it from the oven. Leave it in its wrapping for at least 15 minutes. ¶ Incorporate into your dough ingredients such as raisins, currants, or other dried fruits.

Serving Suggestions

Irish soda bread can be served warm or at room temperature. ¶ Some people slice the bread; others break it into chunks with their hands. ¶ The marriage of butter and jam, jelly, or marmalade to Irish soda bread was made in heaven.

Unseasoned Stocks

~§ As good cooks know, the difference in quality between a home-made stock and its factory-produced counterpart is significant. Making stocks from scratch is worth the effort.

Because stocks freeze well, you can save time by preparing them in quantity. Then you'll have them on hand to serve as the base for myriad creations — including soups, stews, and sauces.

People who cook only one type of cuisine (French, for instance) can season their stocks when they make them. However, if you prepare dishes from a variety of ethnic cuisines, you should make unseasoned stocks. Otherwise, you will be imbuing — for example — the French philosophy of seasoning into *soupa avgolemono,* a Greek specialty. That, of course, precludes you from cooking authentic ethnic dishes. To eliminate that problem, I specify unseasoned stocks in the recipes of this book. The tailor-made seasonings for each preparation are incorporated into the recipe.

Should you have to use a seasoned stock in one of these recipes, it is essential that you make adjustments for the type and quantity of the various flavoring agents (including salt) that are contained in the substitute stock. And, remember, the dish will be only as good as the stock you use.

How to Make Unseasoned Beef, Veal, and Chicken Stocks

Note: Beef, veal (calf), and chicken stocks should be made at least one day in advance. This gives the fat a chance to rise to the top of the stock and solidify, thereby facilitating its removal. For best results, use a minimum of 2 pounds of beef or veal bones or 1 pound of chicken bones. The height of the pot should be almost twice that of the batch of bones inside it.

195

1. Place the bones in a pot. Cover beef and veal bones with 2 inches and chicken bones with 1 inch of cold tap water.

2. Bring the water to a boil. Reduce the heat and simmer the preparation, uncovered, for 15 minutes. Skim the scum off the surface.

3. Simmer the stock, partially covered, for at least 2 hours for the beef and veal bones and at least 1 hour for the chicken bones.

4. Turn off the heat. Discard the bones. Strain the slightly cooled stock through a fine sieve or through several layers of cheesecloth into one or more warmed storage jars.

How to Make Unseasoned Fish Stock

Note: Fish stock can be made immediately before you plan to use it — or it can be stored for future use.

1. Put the fish bones and, if you have them, the heads and tails into the pot. Barely cover them with cold tap water.

2. Bring the water to a boil. Reduce the heat and simmer the stock, uncovered, for 15 to 20 minutes. Skim the scum off the surface as necessary.

3. Turn off the heat. Discard the fish parts. Strain the stock through a fine sieve or several layers of cheesecloth into a heat-resistant container. (If you plan to strain it directly into storage jars, let the stock cool slightly and warm the jars to keep them from cracking.)

Storage Tips and Guidelines

¶ The maximum suggested storage period for beef, veal, and chicken stock is four days in the refrigerator, a month in the frozen food compartment, and several months in a 0° F freezer. For fish stock, cut these periods in half.

¶ The storage life of refrigerated beef, veal, and chicken stocks can be extended indefinitely if you simmer them for 10 minutes at least once every four days.

¶ The fat layer serves as a protective seal. Do not discard it until you are ready to use the stock. (However, if you plan to freeze the stock for more than a month, remove the fat. Otherwise, the fat might become rancid.)

¶ To thaw frozen stock, let it stand in the refrigerator for one to two days. Or, if the stock is stored in a wide-mouthed jar, it can easily be removed from its container and thawed in a pan over low heat.

Additional Keys to Success

Use uncooked bones. Those from cooked meat have lost much of their sought-after flavor.

¶ The ingredients for a stock must be fresh. Your nose is the best judge.

¶ Beef, veal, and chicken stocks will be more gelatinous if made with the bones of an older animal — or with the bones from the head, neck, shoulder, tail, or limbs.

¶ Beef, veal, and chicken stock will be more delicately and subtly flavored if made with the bones of a younger animal — or with the bones from the breast, ribs, or middle of the back.

¶ Beef, veal, and chicken bones should be sawed or cracked into small segments in order to maximize flavor extraction. If the butcher will not perform this service for you, use a meat saw to cut the bones. Ideally, the maximum dimension of each piece should be less than 2 inches.

¶ Chicken stock should not be made from backbones that still have pieces of liver clinging to them. Unless you scrape away that organ meat, the stock will develop the unwanted flavor of overcooked liver.

¶ Fish stock will have a more delicate and subtle flavor if made with the parts of a nonoily fish (sole, for example) as opposed to those of an oily one (mackerel, for instance).

¶ Fish stock must not be cooked too long lest it develop an undesirable taste and odor.

¶ Never start cooking bones in hot water. By beginning the process in cold water, you maximize flavor extraction.

¶ As a stock sits in the refrigerator, its nonfat solids sink. If you want to use only the clear portion of the stock, carefully ladle it out of the container while leaving the sediment-infused bottom portion of the stock behind.

Index

Index

✑ An asterisk (*) indicates that the ingredient is listed in the "Variations on a Theme" section of the recipe. See "Recipes by Categories" beginning on page *xi* for classifications such as "Country of Origin."

⅋ About the Author

Howard Hillman is the author of *Kitchen Science* (Houghton Mifflin), *The Cook's Book* (Avon), *The Book of World Cuisines* (Penguin), *The Diner's Guide to Wines* (Hawthorn), and a series of dining-out guidebooks to major cities. All told, he has written more than twenty books.

His books have been critically acclaimed, selected by book clubs, and heralded as "Outstanding Reference Books" by both the *Library Journal* and the American Library Association.

Hillman has written for such noted publications as the *New York Times*, the *Washington Post*, the *Chicago Tribune*, the *Wall Street Journal*, *The Cook's Magazine*, and *Food & Wine*. He has critically rated restaurants for America's largest newspaper.

His culinary journeys have taken him more than a million miles to more than a hundred countries. Hillman has lectured on television and at the university level, has been a guest on numerous radio and television talk shows, and maintains a multi-thousand-volume food and wine reference library.

Hillman has served as president of the National Academy of Sports and as vice president of the American Film Theatre. He received his M.B.A. from the Harvard Business School in 1961.